The Soul Family

A Guide to Karmic relationships, Soulmates, Soul Tribes, and Twin Flames

Alexx Shaw

Published by VARDO, LLC, 2023.

While every precaution has been taken in the preparation of this book, the publisher assumes no responsibility for errors or omissions, or for damages resulting from the use of the information contained herein.

THE SOUL FAMILY

First edition. December 1, 2023.

ISBN: 979-8215395172

Written by Alexx Shaw.

Definitions of Recurring Terms

Ego

The mind; mind-stuff; thoughts; what we filter things through; what we utilize every day to create thoughts and emotions; what creates duality; perception

3D/3D Reality

The plane of existence we live in day-to-day; the world we live in via the ego; what we see around us when we are functioning on a human, egoic level

5D

The energetic plane of existence; the dimension where we connect to things energetically; where the Higher Self communicates from

4D

The bridge between the 5D plane of energetic existence and 3D reality as linear time

Higher Self

The universe; universal energy; the true nature beyond Ego; what gives us guidance through "channeling;" where the clair senses lay; "intuition"

Divine Timing

Universal "time" dictated by the Higher Self which corresponds to a linear timeframe so the Ego can understand it

The Proof is in the Particles

We are the universe manifested in physical form

This statement isn't New Age woo-woo, but a scientific fact, and before we get into the nitty-gritty of Soul Families, it's important to first understand our own "purpose" within the universe, for there cannot be a Soul Family without the general knowledge of their *raison d'être*.

On a physical level, 99% of the human body is made up of hydrogen, carbon, nitrogen, and oxygen atoms. The other 1% are essential elements to support life. The majority of these cells regenerate every seven to fifteen years, but the particles that make up these cells have been around for millions of millennia: the hydrogen atoms were produced during the Big Bang; carbon, nitrogen, and oxygen atoms from burning stars; and heavy elements (the 1%) from exploding stars. All of these particles only make up 20% mass of each cell, and the remaining space around them, which creates the other 80% mass of a cell, is made up of energy. If we were to shrink our cells down to only physical particles, our entire body would be the size of a particle of dust, and if we were to do this to every person alive, the entire human race would fit into the volume of a sugar cube. We are literally walking, talking balls of energy that look like solid things.

On a scientific level, it began with Plato speaking about "seen and unseen energies," and was popularized and proven by Einstein and the most known equation in the world: $E = mc^2$, or the mass-energy equivalence. This equation, that energy equals mass times the speed of light squared, simply states that energy and mass (or matter), are interchangeable.

Einstein's theory of special relativity expresses that mass and energy are the same physical entity, and therefore can be changed into one another. This corresponds to a body at rest which has the potential to transform into another body. So for example, the mass of an undisturbed rock has the potential to become energy in a different form. If we blow up the rock, the energy released can then become a different rock or a quartz countertop. It's easy to think about it in forms where like becomes like, but what if I took it a step further and said that rock that we blew up could then become a human?

Quantum Physics shows us we are ONE

In 1935, Albert Einstein, Boris Podolsky, and Nathan Rosen wrote a paper discussing strongly correlated quantum states of particles and their interactions with one another. They found that when two particles are strongly correlated, they lose their individual states and instead share one unified state. They posed that one could place these strongly correlated particles at opposite ends of the universe, and they would still share the same state. They called it the EPR Paradox, but after reading the hypothesis, physicist Erwin Schrödinger coined the term "entanglement." At the time, the three scientists were baffled by this theory, because it nullified the idea of cause and effect, and it was so crazy to posture, that even Einstein died not believing it was real.

In 1950, Chien-Shiung Wu and Irving Shaknov found strangely linked behavior between a pair of photons that correlated to the EPR Paradox, but it wasn't until 1964 that physicist John Stewart Bell created a mathematical equation that could be tested. In 1981, French physicist Alain Aspect was the first to test and prove that Bell's equation and Einstein-Podolsky-Rosen were correct in their theories, and that quantum entanglement actually does exist.

Quantum entanglement is a physical phenomenon that occurs when a group of particles cannot be measured independently from one another because they act in identical manners no matter the distance between them. That means that if a group of particles is separated and half of them are flown to the other side of the world, both sets of particles will still act identically at the exact same moment in time regardless of what you do to either set of them. The energy is entangled with itself, even though it is in multiple distinct mass forms, and acts accordingly without any interaction with itself in another physical location. This would be like if you and your friend lived across the country from one another and at the exact same time both began doing jumping jacks with zero differences between the two actions: including wingspan, space between your legs, direction you're facing, and even sweat output. And if someone came by and hit your arm, your friend's arm would move in the identical way at the exact moment in time that yours did. This analogy is focused on two large supposed mass bodies being entangled with one another, but both of those bodies contain 50 trillion cells each. As stated above, each one of those cells is 80% pure energy and 20% physical mass which is ultimately energy in its most elementary form. Therefore, if just two of us have 100 trillion cells between us, how can anyone believe that we are not intrinsically and fundamentally entangled with one another.

On October 1, 1990, twenty universities around the world began mapping all of the genes of the human genome. It became the world's largest collaborative biological project which lasted thirteen years until 85% of it was completed. Known as the *Human Genome Project*, it is a mosaic of genes sequenced from a small number of individuals, not representing a sole person, since the vast majority of genomes are identical in everyone. After all, we are physically pretty much all the same. The purpose of the Human Genome Project was to gain insight on why diseases appear and how to properly eradicate them, since the belief was that our DNA is coded with all information, and plugging in external information can change it. But what geneticists did not expect, was that our DNA could not explain our behavior. More easily said, our DNA showed there is in fact a difference between nature and nurture.

Not having found the precoding for our genes led to a new study called *epigenetics* ("above the gene"), in which behaviors and environment are studied in order to gauge how these changes can affect the way genes work. Epigenetic changes do not physically alter the DNA sequence, but they do affect how the body reads these DNA sequences. Epigenetic changes are also reversible within the body, and can turn genes on and off or alter the expression of a gene. For example, if someone has been severely stressed out for the majority of their life, this can turn cancer genes on, regardless of whether they have a predisposition to it genetically. Your environment affects your behavior, and your behavior can affect your DNA. This is epigenetics at work.

The entire point of this story is to bring you into the field of Quantum Biology and a phenomenon known as *Quantum Coherence*, which is a close relative to Entanglement. Quantum Coherence shows how all objects have wave-like properties, but when the waves are split into two, they will interfere with each other in order to create a single state that represents both waves. A different way of putting this, is that Quantum Coherence occurs when an electron interacts with more than one molecule at a time, and enters into a multi-state existence.

This was proven via an experiment with marine algae and photosynthesis, whereby each chlorophyll molecule of a plant spins, rotates, and vibrates at the exact frequency and wavelength together, turning the sun's electromagnetic energy into chemical energy. They do this by sending the sun's energy through multiple pathways simultaneously, and finding the quickest path to completion. Biophysicist Greg Scholes compares it to driving home in rush hour traffic, taking one out of three possible routes. You're guessing at which route will be fastest, but in quantum mechanics, you can take all three routes simultaneously, leading you to always choose the quickest way.

What does this have to do with genes and epigenetics? Let me give you an example regarding mass meditation. In the 1980's during the Lebanon war, 1,000 people in Jerusalem meditated on world peace, and subsequently, war deaths in Lebanon decreased by 75%. Also on the days that mass meditations were held, general crime rates and destructive happenings lowered around the world. Called the *Maharishi Effect*, over fifty studies have been done in the last fifty years measuring crime rates in the areas surrounding the meditators. Published in the *Journal of Criminal Justice*, cities in which 1% of the population practiced group Transcendental Meditation showed to drop crime rates by an average of 1-2% both immediately and within the following five years in comparison to the control group cities.

When a large group of people come together regardless of their genetics and epigenetic environments, put their intentions on the same goal and enter into a state of meditation, they physically change the world. This is cohesion. It does not matter your gender; age; culture; environment; genes; history; physical attributes; health issues; or beliefs. You do not have to individually try to spread your message, protest, or affect others with your words. With meditation, you are entering into a state of Quantum Cohesion (multiple states at the same time), syncing with other energy around you, and directly altering 3D reality in the quickest and most competent way possible.

String Theory delineates Ego

I'm not going to get too deep into String Theory because it is just layering theories on top of theories. Nothing in String Theory has been proven, thus far, however, it's best to use this science to explain what Ego is. I want to introduce you to the idea of the *Holographic Principle*, which states that the universe is a vast hologram: a two-dimensional surface that appears to have depth.

Mathematically, the Holographic Principle works out, since the laws of physics can be described mathematically utilizing two dimensions instead of three. It also helps to explain how gravity works on a very small scale, for example, in a black hole (yes, this is considered a small scale in physics).

In previous theories, once matter falls into a black hole, it disappears. But as energy cannot be destroyed nor created, physicists couldn't explain what was happening to the matter. With the Holographic Principle, this paradox is solved by theorizing that the matter is not in fact destroyed, but rather the information contained in the matter is smeared across the boundary of the black hole.

On the quest to understand how gravity works and what it looks like, String Theorists claim that this two-dimensional universe is actually just made up of information which is encoded on the boundaries of the universe. As a CD is coded with information of music and playing it makes everything cohesive and "real," when we are able to decode the information of the universe (such as positions and velocities of physical objects), we perceive it as cohesive. Basically, when you remove gravity from the equation (by making the universe flat), space becomes a side effect of particle interactions as opposed to the main ingredient of the cosmos. Therefore, everything we see and experience is an illusion.

Let me say that again: everything we see and experience is an illusion, and this perfectly sums up the Ego. The Holographic Principle asserts that the universe is in fact just an illusion that's being perceived as something other than what it really is. By utilizing perception and filters of the mind, we see everything in a three-dimensional form with large, solid physical objects; holes that rip through space; and more importantly, as separate and different from everything else instead of one cohesive whole. This is identical to the 3D realm we live our daily lives in.

The innate problem with the Holographic Principle is that if the universe is "coded" within a boundary, there needs to be someone or something that can decode it. It sets up a dichotomy of duality and makes it so that Ego is required in order to understand how the universe works. But as everything is made up of energy and we are in fact the universe manifested in physical form, we should not need Ego to understand how it works, because we *are* how it works. Stating that the universe is coded, is equivalent to saying that there is a personified God whose entire mission and purpose is to take care of us humans, as if we're the most important things. But the universe is not created *for us*; the universe is created *as us, by us*.

❊❊❊

There are scientifically, four fundamental forces at work in the universe: electromagnetic force (a physical reaction between electrically charged particles); strong nuclear forces (an attraction force between protons and neutrons); weak nuclear forces (radioactive decay of certain nuclei); and gravity. These four fundamental forces were elucidated by Einstein in his theory of special relativity ($E = mc^2$).

For over 100 years, scientists have searched for ways to unite energy from electromagnetic force with the other three forces since Einstein's theory showed that mass warped four dimensional space-time. Since we cannot see these four dimensions, we attribute the motion of a large mass (like a planet) to the force of gravity, but the electromagnetic force does not fit in.

Two theories surfaced on the existence of a fifth dimension in which electromagnetism and gravity unify. However, in order for the fifth dimension to allow gravity to outweigh electromagnetism as it does (electromagnetic force is over 1,000 times stronger than gravity), there must be a curvature of a fifth dimension so immense that it's smaller than the size of an atom, curls up on itself, and is completely invisible to the human eye. The fifth dimension is hence contemplated to be a micro dimension that is made up of pure energy.

You'll hear in spirituality that the 5D plane is where love, compassion, and the highest "good" reside. You'll hear that astral beings from the fifth dimension will show up here on Earth. You'll hear that the fourth dimension contains dark vibrations and energy, but if you can transcend to the fifth dimension with self-love, then you'll be safe. The amount of things that are circulating out there about the 5D are all wrong; I'm just going to say that flat out. And why are they all wrong? Because they all have to do with 3D constructs of duality as created by the Ego. Let me put it this way: You cannot state that a dimension of pure energy with no physical form has any sense of consciousness in the manner of Ego.

If we think about living in 3D reality and the 5D as pure energy, the fourth dimension is like the bridge between worlds. As a three-dimensional object casts a two-dimensional shadow, four-dimensional objects cast a three-dimensional shadow. Therefore:

Pure Energy/Light (5D) ⇨ The area that energy is being shone on (4D) ⇨ The shadow (3D)

-OR-

Our Higher Self ⇨ The Bridge ⇨ Intuition filtered and perceived by Ego

We are a three-dimensional shadow of a different plane of energetic existence. We are constantly getting fed energetic information from this energetic plane, and if we are in touch with our clair senses, we can utilize the Ego to decipher them.

But ultimately, we are nothing but pure energy, and the same energy, at that. We are accustomed to all forms of energy here on Earth, but we have a tendency to compartmentalize and view them as separate from each other instead of as one unified whole. We think about density with regards to energy, and that's because we're able to experience heavily dense objects with our senses: we can touch another's hand; smell a rose; hear a band playing music; taste an apple; and see a horse. But we know that light waves are energy, sound waves are energy, and they are invisible to us just as the energy that moves the air is or the particles that make up atoms are. We believe that the sun is energy because we are told that it is, but why do we not recognize that the smallest temperature change against our skin is also energy? Because we cannot see through a wall, we believe it wholeheartedly to be real; to be solid; to be fixed. But the energy that makes up the wall is the same energy that makes up the clouds, and when that wall becomes dilapidated and swallowed up by nature, it too will become clouds or the air or the ocean. Therefore, if everything is made up of energy and energy is interchangeable with everything else, then everything in existence is the same.

I AM

Who are you?

Every time you state that you are something correlated to this 3D world, you are being led by Ego. You are not your name, nor your occupation; your gender, nor your culture; your experiences, nor your pursuits. These are all characteristics of your current manifestation's costume, but they are not *who you are*. Who you are is the same as who I am. Who you are is synonymous with what the chair in your living room is. Who you are is equivalent to whom everyone and what everything is: ONE. We are One because we are all made up of the exact same thing: pure and eternal energy. And if we are pure and eternal oneness energy, all the same, and just differentiate ourselves via Ego, then we are "God." If "God" created the universe and we are "God," then WE created the universe and are the universe.

But how can there be a "we" if "we" are all One? There isn't. The correct phrasing is "I." And if I am not going to associate with egoic constructs, then who are you? I AM. Who am I? I AM. What is that? I AM.

Why am I here if I AM?

As the universe, I AM everything and nothing. I AM always and I AM never. I AM light and I AM dark. I AM good and I AM bad. For it is only through these egoic constructs of duality that everything and nothing can exist simultaneously. Without a mind, there just is. There is no right or wrong, no up or down, no here nor there. *There just is.*

As the universe, there is just "I." And as just "I," I cannot experience myself unless I look at a convoluted reflection of myself. So I created all and none, and I exploded energy into different manifestations, dimensions, and physical masses, including that which can mentally understand itself...that which can transform energy into emotions, and experience "I" through them. Yet, through even the small lens of emotions there are infinite things I can experience about myself, and so Ego gets pushed to the forefront and I forget who I AM. I forget I AM the universe and I see "I" as "we, you, he, she, they, it, that, those, this," and everything else that separates me further from myself.

The majority of experienced emotions tend to be perceived as painful, which is why happiness is so fleeting for most. As a species, we have evolved to view and use the mind more than anything else. It is what has kept us safe against predators; it is what has allowed us to grow technologically; and it is what allows us to understand things. But the Ego is and has always been a tool to aid us; it was never meant to be the sole sense we trust. The conundrum lies in the sense that we cannot fully experience ourself as the universe unless Ego is broken down and utilized as a tool to do so. Ego in today's world makes us not only forget who I AM, but creates separation; expectations; false importance; value systems; differing moralities; fear and phobias; mental illness and addictions; hurtful thought patterns; war and destruction; and a consistent duality that we base our lives on. Because Ego has become the main motivation to do anything, the universe (i.e. the Higher Self) needed to create a link back to Source. And that link comes in the form of certain lessons in each manifestation.

Perspective and purpose aren't real

Ego gives us perception and perspective that we view as "facts." When we view the color orange, we all know that it's orange, but how do you know that how you see orange is the same way that I see it? I could see it as your color "blue," but was taught that blue is called "orange."

The internet and news channels are the worst architects of "facts," for we can have a perspective and always find multiple outlets to agree with us, making us hold concrete that those beliefs are "facts." For example, the division of political ideas and ideologies creates such a huge chasm between humans, yet it is a literal partition of perspective that we have labeled as "fact." The Right and Left both claim things and show "proof" via statistics, polls, images, videos, data, and opinion. They tell you that the other side is "wrong;" they pump you with emotional priming and religious acumen; speak about how this action will take away your freedom; or this action isn't "fair." But both of these sides are functioning off of their own beliefs, their own agendas, their own perspectives and Ego. Both sides want victory, and neither side cares how they get it. Therefore, there can never be true honesty in general because "truth" is personal perspective. Truth is Ego.

One of the false truths we live by is that of time and linear time. In our 3D reality, we view the passage of time via birth, growth, decay, and death. We talk about cycles, and fear our mortality. But mortality is merely perspective; it's the Ego not wanting to let go of all we believe to know in this manifestation. Imagine if we were able to shut our Ego down and only use it to discern when we requested it to do so. We would no longer be afraid of "death" because fear itself is created by the Ego; the concept of death is created by the Ego; time is created by the Ego; and Ego death would have already occurred by our own choice. We would understand that cycles are also just perspective, for energy cannot be created nor destroyed, and is always in a state of transition and expansion. When we see Autumn leaves change color and fall only to be rebloomed in Spring, we perceive it to be a cycle, as it happens every year. But when it's broken down into its most basic element, we see that even the cycle of seasons are perspective: the leaves, blooms, and tree itself are simply physical mass that are made up of energy; the passage of time isn't real; and the death of those leaves are quietly transitioning energy to a different area. When the Ego is so confined that we can sense and see energy as I AM, it doesn't appear in physical mass or in cycles. It is all around us, it makes up everything, and it is us because we have created it. As I AM, we are everything personified, everything that's ever existed, that hasn't existed, that will exist, that can't exist, that does exist. We have to look past the Ego's sense of duality in order to recognize that we are everything and nothing simultaneously, because since we are the ONLY, there is nothing else.

On the same note, it is only through Ego forgetting that we are Source do we look for "purpose" in our life. Egoic purpose comes in the manifestation of occupation, family, location, appearance, friends, partners, philanthropy, and anything else tied to what we believe or have been taught we should be doing within this incarnation. As the universe, our entire purpose is to experience every moment so that we may truly see ourself.

This isn't to say that there is no enjoyment from the false purposes we have created, but when we step back and observe our life, what is truly the point? Separate from the Ego for a moment, breathe, and look deeply. The things that feel like nirvana are not attached to Ego: unconditional love, peace, non-attachment. These are the things that are being felt on a purely energetic level and not filtered through the mind, mostly because they are coming in through the Higher Self. Whereas the more surface gratifications are all attached to the mind: getting a promotion, praise from others, a new romantic relationship. All of the things that we chase throughout our life have been told to us that they're what we're "supposed" to do, or "should" do/have/acquire/feel/aspire to. In our 3D reality, we obviously need to make money because we cannot eat without money, which ultimately kills the body. But the amount of stress we put on ourselves on how much money we make, or how big our house is, or that we need to get married by x age are all absolute nonsense. For some of us, we spend our life searching for our purpose, never knowing what we're "supposed" to be doing, and feeling insignificant or like failures when others judge us based on their own programmed egoic perspectives. For others, we spend our life hyper-obsessed with our jobs or finding a partner, leaving us perpetually engaged in the Ego and never attending to our actual needs, but instead wasting this manifestation.

The Ego likes to create the emotions that we feel throughout the day; fluctuating minute-by-minute and distinguishing these emotions between "good" and "bad." But if our emotions are attached to any form of duality, then it is not I AM experiencing emotions, but rather the Ego playing tricks. And when the Ego plays tricks, we are not fulfilling the entire reason we manifested ourself. If for nothing else, let this be confirmation that whatever purpose you think you have or need to have, it is a false societal, personal, and egoic construct that means absolutely nothing.

Just because we are I AM does not mean we don't each have our own Egos. We experience things collectively to get a full emotional experience of what we've created. Everything that happens in your life, you have created – after all, you are the universe. Stop and think 'why?' Why did you create the situation that occurred? What was it trying to show you? What did it teach you? What did you want or need that you didn't have until the situation was created? Every single situation that happens in your world is created by YOU; because you are the universe. This is manifestation in its truest form. You created the situation via pure, unadulterated energy, but then the Ego got in the way and reacted to the situation. Therefore, you literally reacted to your own creation, because remember, without Ego, there is no action nor reaction. There just is. Now here is what is important to remember: each situation in which you react, you created in order to *learn a lesson*.

Core Karmic Lessons

What are Core Karmic lessons?

Core Karmic lessons are the crux of forgetting who I AM. They are what all other Karmic lessons stem from. They are the creators of "symptom" Karmic lessons.

Core Karmic lessons are what the Ego attempts to ingrain deeply so that it can remain in control. They are the lessons that the Ego sublimates and covers up so it doesn't get destroyed. They are what we attempt to "fix" about ourselves, but since we are doing it with the Ego, we can only understand that we have said "issue" to "fix."

Core Karmic lessons are those that our family show us at the beginning of every human incarnation the Higher Self has. They are what every member of the Soul Family are attempting to trigger so that we may begin to heal. They are what ultimately cause Ego Degradation if they are unearthed too quickly or triggered before we are mentally ready.

Core Karmic lessons are solely human burdens. They are hardships for the mind. They are censored by the Ego which creates falsities in the forms of perception, dualism, emotions, and reactions in order to not resuscitate them.

Core Karmic lessons are what drive us to ruminate, obsess, and go into egoic hyper-drive. They are what push the Ego to look outwardly for love, validation, and worth. They are why we choose to blame, hate, judge, gaslight, and focus on material possessions.

Core Karmic lessons are the entire reason I AM has manifested as human, in order to experience itself through emotions and overcome the consignment to oblivion.

There are three Core Karmic lessons

Though there are a seemingly never-ending plethora of Karmic lessons that I AM can experience as human, there are only three that are Core Karmic lessons, and it could take a few, hundreds, or thousands of incarnations to truly learn just one of them, dependent on how much the Ego can be tamed. Core Karmic lessons are of course not linear, and if I AM decides to manifest again as a human after this current body deteriorates, it may not be with the same Core Karmic lesson as is present.

The three Core Karmic lessons are that of self-worth, self-love, and non-attachment. Each of these lessons are the base root of all "symptoms" of other Karmic lessons encountered, and it is each Ego's responsibility to figure out which Core Karmic lesson they are dealing with in this incarnation and begin to dismantle the distorted stories the mind tells itself. Acknowledgement is the first step, always.

Self-worth

Self-worth as a Core Karmic lesson tends to be in those that have lived through a lot of neglect or abandonment as a child. It may feel as though there is something innately "wrong" about your Being, and the Ego may find "proof" to such via stories to itself regarding "why" a parent was neglectful; why a parent abandoned; or why a parent "didn't care."

Those with self-worth as a Core Karmic lesson are generally very open in their clair senses, using clairsentience (clear feeling) as their primary way of determining and predicting the needs of those around them. However, since they have a lack of their own self-worth, these Egos will give and give, depleting themselves and not knowing how to say "no." They may have dealt with sexual abuse when young, and/or become sexually over-active as they grew up (especially females), thinking that it was the only way in which people would accept them. They may have felt completely socially awkward growing up, or have social anxiety disorder as an adult. They may become addicts, or lovers of addicts, co-dependently trying to fix those who are socially looked down upon. Those with self-worth as their Core Karmic lesson are usually terrible with setting their own boundaries and desire to be needed instead of wanted, since they do not believe that there is anything in them that is worth sticking around for.

Some Karmic "symptoms" of self-worth as a Core Karmic lesson may present themselves as follows:

- Abandonment issues
- Addictions or attraction to addicts
- Needing to be the priority within intimate

relationships
- Anxiety about how you appear to the outside world and/or social anxiety
- Undercurrent of continuous fear and/or phobias
- Codependency/Needing to be needed
- Lack of boundary setting/not knowing how to set boundaries
- Heightened clair senses, especially clairsentience
- False outward pride to the point of detriment
- Narcissistic tendencies
- Putting yourself in precarious situations without concern or even a thought about your well-being
- Heightened sexuality

Self-love

Self-love as a Core Karmic lesson tends to be in those that grew up with a lot of criticism or expectations from parents or primary care givers. It may feel as though you have to "prove" yourself and everything you do in order to gain approval. It is akin to the work/reward system, but the "reward" in this case, is love. This can also be seen in adults who reward themselves with addictive behaviors (shopping, drugs/drinking, gambling, etc.) when they feel they have "accomplished" something (e.g. "I've had a long week, so I'm going to enjoy a night out drinking").

Those with self-love as their Core Karmic lesson are usually very gregarious towards the outside world. Though they may not feel comfortable internally, they are amazing at putting on masks and being whatever they gauge others want them to be.

They are fun to be around, the life of the party, and possibly appear stuck-up in certain situations. They also may need a lot of alone time in order to recuperate after being around many people, since they are simply pretending to love everything as much as they seem to. They could love to gossip in order to get the attention off of themselves and look "more interesting" than they feel. Those with self-love as a Core Karmic lesson tend to be Type A personalities, and may have severe underlying anxiety.

Some Karmic "symptoms" of self-love as a Core Karmic lesson may present themselves as follows:

- Physical OCD, perfectionism, or physical tics
- Anxiety about how you appear to the outside world and/or social anxiety
- Addictive behaviors as a reward system
- Type A personality
- Workaholism or severe laziness
- Crippling fear of failure
- Always feeling like you have to "prove" yourself
- Parental issues of the opposite sex ("Mommy/Daddy issues")
- Repressed sexuality
- Extreme judgements about others
- Difficulty with impulsivity control
- False arrogance

Non-attachment

Non-attachment is the most interesting of the Core Karmic lessons because it is both the first and last Core Karmic lesson I AM manifests, and aspects of it are addressed within every human manifestation. If the Higher Self creates a "new" human incarnation, their Core Karmic lesson will be of non-attachment. This will be seen as needing to become equanimous with all the egoic pleasures humans encounter. Non-attachment is what all religions and philosophies talk about regarding good vs. evil.

In the first incarnation as a human, those with non-attachment as a Core Karmic lesson may look like the most "shallow" of Egos, obsessed with physical comforts, outward appearances, other Egos, and everything external to the Self, not because there is a lack of self-love or self-worth, but simply a pure attachment to Ego (people, places, things, ideas, stature, etc.). As the last incarnation, this may arrive as full composure and a detachment from everything external, which is seen in only a few throughout history; or those we have called "Enlightened." However, we have to be careful with naming other Egos "enlightened," for the majority of them still had attachments of some form. Non-attachment in some form can be taught in every human incarnation, especially during any form of Ego Degradation.

Those with non-attachment as their Core Karmic lesson don't have a particular way that they appear. Think of most Gurus and religious figures, product influencers, cult leaders, politicians, and Hollywood film industry bigwigs. They of course don't all have non-attachment as a Core Karmic lesson, but they are the ones where it's easier to see the pattern.

Non-attachment is a difficult Core Karmic lesson to see because society teaches humans that we need to be attached to things in order to be "happy" or "normal." Attachment can be a cover-up for another Core Karmic lesson, filling the hole with possessions or things that externally validate. Also, if you have manifested your Twin Flame in this incarnation, non-attachment *cannot be your Core Karmic lesson*, for you will always be attached to your Twin.

Some Karmic "symptoms" of non-attachment as a Core Karmic lesson may present themselves as follows:

- Excessive jealousy in all forms
- Hoarding
- Selfishness towards attaining goals, accomplishments, or power
- Abuse of power
- Entitlement or the feeling of "deserving"
- Righteousness or zeal over personal beliefs or ideas
- Expecting others to "do as you say, not as you do"
- Vices, thrill seeking, or pornography addiction
- Obsession with physical pleasures
- Surrounding yourself with only those who can "further you" in some way
- Wanting things your way without regard or concern for anything or anyone else
- A crippling fear of death or the unknown

❋❋❋

It is important to note that when we are still young adults, it is probable that we may confuse our Core Karmic lesson with another one. There are some that show multiple "symptom" lessons from multiple groups, but it is not really until the Ego steadies slightly in the body's thirties that the mind can accurately see what it needs to heal. Also, those with a self-worth Core Karmic lesson may feel that they do not love themselves, but when it's fully unpacked and looked at, it can be seen that the root cause is in fact self-worth. The same can be said about those who have a Core Karmic lesson of self-love and surround themselves with material possessions in order to present themselves as "better-than" they feel. Though they may feel like their Core Karmic lesson is that of non-attachment, when everything is scrutinized, it becomes apparent that the lesson is in fact self-love. Be honest with yourself regarding how your Ego *truly feels* about itself and your Higher Self as a form of universal energy. This will be your guiding light.

The Soul Family

The purpose of the Soul Family

The term "Soul Family" is a very misguided term, because it makes us think that we are connected to them via the Soul. But there is no such thing as a Soul, since everything is One and we just delineate difference through Ego. Therefore, your Soul Family is created by I AM, or the Higher Self.

There is a lot of information out there regarding the Soul Family and the participants in it. Some delineate it by Soul Family, Soul Group, Soulmate, and Twin Flame. Some define it as the Soul, Oversoul, Soul Families, Soul Collectives, and Parallel Souls. This book depicts the members as Karmic, Soulmates, Soul Tribe, and Twin Flames, which are all part of the entirety of the Soul Family. Think about a Soul Family in the same vein as a "traditional" family:

1. The Twin Flame would be your spouse, always connected in some form, and the closest to you. You are a single unit together.
2. Soulmates would be your children, with you for many years and learning from one another, but ultimately they go along their own paths.
3. The Soul Tribe would be your parents, always there for support and someone to lean on.
4. Karmic relationships would be your extended family,

scattered about here and there, coming into your life every so often for a reason.

All of the Soul Family members trigger us into remembering who "I" truly am by hitting the Ego in certain ways and teaching the lessons the Higher Self decided to learn in this manifestation. If we do not learn those lessons in this life, we transmute our energy into the next manifestation and learn them there with different incarnations of the Soul Family.

The Soul Family does not follow us from life-to-life; mainly because nothing exists outside of I AM, and therefore, all energy used to create the Soul Family is the same as that which we are manifesting as ourselves. Those who we call Soul Family members, are simply demonstrations created by us for us. How we have pre-decided to create our Soul Family comes in different forms in each life dependent on how we manifest. For example, if you are a heterosexual female in this current manifestation, you may designate the majority of your soulmates as heterosexual males. However, in another human incarnation, you may be a homosexual male and incarnate your Twin Flame as the same. Sexual preference is the least of any concern, but as preferences are part of the human experience regarding emotions, you will manifest at some points in all gender bodies with all gender preferences, and at certain times with no predilections.

The entire purpose of the Soul Family is to help you learn the lessons you incarnated here in order to experience, and to remind you that you are in fact I AM. With every Soul Family member you encounter, you get closer and closer to reintegrating as pure universal energy and dissipating back into the cosmos having experienced itself through all emotions as a human. This isn't to say that humanity is the top tier of existence; remember that there are infinite ways for the universe to materialize. As I AM, you are boundless, immeasurable, unending, perpetual, and incalculable. And all of that energy is coursing inside your human frame, being shelled by the mind which believes it has full power...until the Soul Family members aid in causing Ego Degradation and prompting you to recall your unbounded and absolute power.

Soul Families can be exhausting

There are times that your Soul Family can be utterly exhausting and draining. You connect with your Soul Family in the 5D – the plane of pure energy – and this is why you have such a magnetizing pull to them. But living in the 3D plane, the Ego tends to inundate people with pointless directives that overtake them at times. Whether this is through emotions, thoughts, ideas, or beliefs, if your Soul Family member is overly concerned with egoic ideologies, you will feel it sap your energy.

Sometimes, a fight with a Karmic may make you feel like you're going through a bout of narcolepsy, whereby every word they're speaking to you, you can barely keep your eyes open. Other times, a Soulmate will be spewing their diatribe regarding a dualistic surface topic and you will need to distance yourself for a few days in order to regain your energy. And occasionally, your Ego will get the best of you and pull you so deeply into your emotions, that your Twin Flame will require a nap just to recalibrate their frequency. The reason for all of this is because your Soul Family is not meant to be experienced in solely the realm of the 3D, and this 3D egoic energy is pulling the frequencies down. Of course, we need the Ego to filter and delineate meaning and reason for all energetic things (remember that the 5D casts a 3D shadow), but the Ego is not the main drawing factor to your Soul Family. The Ego is what needs to be broken by your Soul Family.

If you think about the times in which you've sat with members of your Soul Family, just basking in one another's energies in the peaceful bliss of quiet, you'll realize that when you're on the same frequency as one another, the feeling of comfort is prevalent. Of course, the Soul Family's job is to teach you lessons and remind you that you are I AM, so clearly you cannot solely surround yourself with delightful feeling energy all of the time. But if we can learn to separate from the ego with non-attachment, not be concerned regarding the outcome of any situation, and protect our own energy field, we won't be as depleted working with our Soul Family.

If you're finding yourself being burned out by any Soul Family members, remember that it's because you are currently in a higher vibrational frequency than they, and their Ego is attempting to drag your energy to a lower plane. If you sense that your Soul Family member is having the same reaction to you, the sentiment is equivalent: check in with yourself and see what's going on that you are not encompassing high frequencies. Most importantly, be honest with your Soul

Family about letting you know when you're exhausting them and vice versa.

With the above being said, not everyone you meet is in the Soul Family. Most spiritualists who discuss I AM will tell you that every single person you encounter is created to teach lessons, and therefore are part of the Soul Family. This is not true. Yes, you create all people, animals, plants, things, matter, etc., and you create them in your 3D reality, but it does not mean that every one of them is there to jog your memory about who you are. The universe cannot fully experience itself if it is solely dealing with Soul Family members. Firstly, you would lead an incredibly arduous life, because Soul Families are painful to deal with. Secondly, what a boring world the universe would be experiencing if you only manifested specific people. You would quickly understand the "purpose" of life, and would not bother with participating in things the Ego likes (passion, job, family, relationships, attachments, etc.) because you'd be trying to expedite the human experience. And thirdly, the collective experience that you have created is part of what needs to be cleared out through Ego Degradation, and that process in itself is the entire purpose of the Soul Family.

Sometimes you need the ability to sit with someone and watch a stupid movie without feeling overwhelming energy. Sometimes you want to have brunch with someone and laugh at stories from the past. Sometimes you desire the ease and non-attachment of a person next to you where you're just enjoying the moment, expecting and wanting nothing. And you don't need a Karmic lesson by the cashier checking you out at the grocery store. This is the beauty of non-Soul Family members.

Take stock of your Soul Family

Before you begin the individual chapters of the Soul Family members, I suggest getting yourself a notebook and writing down who you believe to be part of your Soul Family. Remember that the members are Karmic, Soulmates, Soul Tribe, and Twin Flames. Apart from your Twin Flame, you can have many members in each group, the majority most likely being Karmic. If you have not met your Twin Flame, don't worry, the chapter on them will be just as important as the rest, and you can prepare yourself for what's to come, if you pre-decided that you wanted to manifest a Twin in this incarnation.

After you've written down your members, maybe you'll find it helpful to explain a little bit about them to yourself for quick future reference: how you met; what they taught you or what you taught them; synchronicities that prove to you that they're a Soul Family member; how they led you to another Soul Family member or to a different life path; how you feel when you're with them; what was going on in your life upon meeting; how you felt after and if the relationship ended. While going through these upcoming chapters, you may realize that who you thought was a Soulmate was in fact a Karmic, or that a Karmic was really a False Flame preparing you for the Twin Flame. You may need to recategorize over and over, cross people off, add people in, and mentally revisit past relationships in order to gain a comprehensive understanding of the lessons you're intended to learn during this manifestation. My hope is that by the end of this book, you have a thorough understanding of how you have curated the people in your Soul Family to show you not only the lessons you pre-designed this incarnation to gain, but that your Soul Family, you, and everything in your world are in fact, the universe manifested in physical form. Your entire Being – everything manifested and not – is the core of I AM.

Karmic Relationships

"THE CONDUCTORS"

The purpose of Karmic relationships

The innate problem with the term "Karmic" is that it delineates *karma*, and this is not the actual case with Karmic relationships. We must understand that all Karma is perspective, which means egoic, for what appears "bad" for you, may in turn be beneficial for another Ego. Experiencing something that you chalk up to karma, may five years later prove to be the most constructive thing for growth as I AM. Wanting karma to affect another Ego who has done you wrong, is merely an attachment to emotions, and ultimately requesting negativity towards yourself, since you are the Only thing.

Karma is a dualistic entity, and as dualism is only created in the mind, it cannot truly exist. We are all the same – I AM – and therefore, what we participate in is collectively the same, just differentiated by Ego. Karmic relationships would therefore be better allocated as *Conductors*, for they guide us towards higher frequency relationships, and lead us out of emotional tribulations that "I" as the universe wants to experience and surmount in this Ego and body. So much so, in fact, that the Higher Self has chosen this specific incarnation to conquer a definitive lesson, and it is the responsibility of this Ego and incarnation to not stand in its own way. Everyone in the world has Karmic relationships, and not just one, but many. We are all One, and therefore have the same lessons to ultimately learn, but we each experience things separately on the 3D plane through the Ego.

Karmic relationships can appear as family, friends, acquaintances, co-workers, intimate relationships, or even someone you briefly meet once. Have you ever heard people say the same thing over and over again about your character or a situation you're currently going through, and then a random stranger may say it and it'll dawn on you what everyone meant? That's an example of how a stranger can be a Karmic; their energy connecting with yours enabled you to understand the beginning of a lesson everyone else was trying to show you. Karmics come in to clear energy and break old patterns in order to make way for higher frequency connections.

Karmic relationships enter your life for two reasons: to teach you Karmic lessons you chose to learn in this incarnation, and to push you forward on your path of remembering that you are the universe by shaking things up, guiding you to expand, or leading you to other Soul Family members. The lessons Karmics show you are a shadow being cast from the 5D into the 3D, and when you encounter a Karmic relationship, there is an immediate reaction from the Ego. You may feel it as repulsion or magnetism, but the gut feeling will be prevalent, because your Higher Self has recognized this person as important for your growth.

Karmics are the most ephemeral members of the Soul Family since they do not stay in your life for a prolonged period of time, and they are the most turbulent of the relationships. They show up in your life when you are at a point of Ego complacency: when the Ego is neither in pain nor pleasure. Karmic relationships will appear in order to get you to expand and jumpstart new lessons you have yet to embark upon. As life is incredibly short in this current manifestation, we do not have the luxury of wasting time by sitting around and being stagnant. If one closes themselves off to the world – having no friends, intimate relationships, or any type of life besides their own myopic bubble – they will have a permanently restless Karmic relationship in their life in the form of an immediate family member, children, or their children's parent. This is to make sure that they are always triggered until they learn to grow. There is no escaping Karmic lessons, so buckle up, embrace them, and try to enjoy the ride.

Karmics are the first member of the Soul Family you encounter

The first Karmic you will encounter will be someone from your immediate family. Whether this is a parent, both parents, a sibling, or all three, at least one of the members of your immediate family is a Karmic relationship for you. If you were raised by your grandparents, they – along with your parents – can be Karmic. If you were adopted, both your biological parents and your adopted parents can be Karmic. If you have step-parents, they are part of it as well. Whoever you chose to be birthed by and the situation in which you decided to grow up, provides you with your *Core Karmic lesson* to be worked on in this incarnation. How you were raised; the issues you developed in childhood (or teenage years); and the struggles you still fight against today, is the most ingrained Karmic lesson I AM will try to move you past in this manifestation. Stemming from this, the Ego no doubt created "symptom" Karmic lessons sprinkled on top.

Whether you had an abusive childhood; a boring childhood; a chaotic childhood; a nondescript one; a good one; a loving family; etc., you have shown yourself the lesson that all Karmics, Soulmates, and your Twin Flame will repeat until you learn and cross it. That's not to say that all Karmics will solely show you this one lesson; Karmic relationships will illuminate your life with a plethora of symptom Karmic lessons as well, but the Core Karmic lesson is the crux of your present expression.

With this all being said, we can detach from the Ego when the next statement is made: children are either Karmic relationships or Soulmates + Karmics. Although you love your child(ren), you have to be prepared to understand and accept that you are in a Karmic relationship with them. And there's nothing wrong with this! In fact, it's a beautiful thing, because you are giving yourself – I AM – the gift of experience through physical manifestation and full cycle participation. What Core Karmic lesson you show your child(ren) is what you as the universe have created for them to learn and heal. It is a literal loop of incarnation:

You choose your parents (which are ultimately you with different Egos) ⇨ you create yourself ⇨ you create your Core Karmic lesson ⇨ your parents show you this lesson ⇨ you create your partner ⇨ you create your child(ren) ⇨ you create their Core Karmic lesson ⇨ you show them that lesson ⇨ they teach you your own Karmic lessons ⇨ they incarnate you again because you are them, just as you are and create everything ⇨ you are shown your new Core Karmic lesson.

There's a certain majesty to and in this process. Now, if you had a child or children without wanting them or trying to have them, your child(ren) become a Karmic lesson for *you*. Of course, Karmic relationships go both ways, but if your child(ren) are manifested as Karmics for you, you may not be the main familial member to show them their Core Karmic lesson.

In the situations in which a child is incarnated as a Karmic lesson for one parent, there tends to be divorce. For example, John may be a Karmic lesson for his mother, in order to teach her to relinquish control since she didn't want to get pregnant for another five years. John's father may be the Core Karmic lesson for John, showing John that he needs to learn self-worth.

A large reason that having children may end a marriage, is because the parents are no longer on the same vibrational frequency as one another. I AM has incarnated a third party (the child) as a Karmic relationship, which throws the energetic dynamic of the familial unit off. If the frequencies can no longer match, and both parents are functioning with a new Karmic relationship that is not one-directional (e.g. both parents are Karmics for the child or vice versa), then there is a deterioration of the egoic family in order to make room for universal and Soul Family lessons. Recognize that as I AM, our one purpose is to experience ourself, and the Higher Self will never allow "I" to be stuck in a situation in which expansion halts. Karmic relationships will either naturally fade away or be ended by the universe, depending on whether you learn the lesson

Katie's story

Katie was born to a narcissistic, bipolar mother and her parents divorced when she was just months old. Katie was then shuffled around between family members to raise her, seeing her biological parents only a few times a week.

As Katie got older, she predominantly lived with her mother, who went from man-to-man seeking validation. Katie was consistently on high alter as to what her mother "needed," tending to those needs as much as she could. Katie's mother married again and had another child with this new man. While pregnant, Katie's mother would state that the new husband and unborn child would provide the family she'd always wanted, while Katie was an unwelcome guest in the house. When Katie was ten years old, her mother decided to move across the country, and informed Katie that she didn't care whether she stayed or went. Katie begged her grandmother – with whom she was close to – to take her in, but after her refusal, Katie moved across the country, feeling like no one wanted her.

As Katie reached her teenage years, her mother's mental illness got worse, and would spend days locked in her bedroom. Katie's step-father lived in his own world and left Katie to take care of and raise her much younger sibling. Katie was consistently walking on eggshells, as she did not know when her mother's mood swings would cause her to become violent, aggressive, or abusive. On certain days, Katie would come home from school to have dishes thrown at her upon entering the house, or the locks to the house changed altogether. Katie was kicked out of the house multiple times for no reason, was told how much everyone in the house hated her, and was slapped around by her step-father if she attempted to de-escalate her mother's moods. A month before her eighteenth birthday, Katie was kicked out of the house permanently.

Six months later, Katie met Matt at a party. The pull was so strong, and they immediately gravitated towards one another. Though Katie had a boyfriend at the time, she cheated on him with Matt and they ended up dating, until one day, Matt dumped Katie out of the blue. Katie felt the same way she had while growing up, and promised herself she would never be left again.

Throughout her early twenties, Katie entered into relationships with people who were insecure, jealous, possessive, and highly emotional. Just like her mother, Katie went from guy-to-guy, not caring if they were in a relationship or not. She relished it if the object of her hunt was attached to another, yet chose Katie over his partner. Katie's goal was to get the other person to "fall in love" with her, then end the relationship. To her, this was personal power: having the ability to push others away before herself being abandoned, whilst on the surface feeling loved.

When Katie was twenty-four years old, Matt appeared at an event she was hosting for work. The same magnetizing pull was there, and they again, began a relationship. When Matt first told Katie he loved her, she attempted to break up with him. But Matt's adamant tears at the prospect, and his insistence for Katie to stay, hit something in her that the other relationships hadn't. Although the other boys had always fought for her, seeing Matt crumpled on the floor as she attempted to abandon him was very reminiscent of her own feelings as a child, and for the first time, Katie felt something shame. From then and there, Katie stopped actively pushing people away.

For the next year and a half, Matt would randomly disappear for days or weeks on end, reappearing and leaving Katie in a whirlwind of emotions. His excuses were different every time, but each time Matt would return, Katie would throw herself into his arms and forgive him. His repetitive promises of never leaving again and words of adoration kept Katie enveloped in the cycle. At times, Matt would introduce Katie to his family and friends, saying that he was going to put a ring on her finger someday, giving Katie hope that she would never have to worry about being left again. She believed herself to be desperately in love.

On Katie's twenty-sixth birthday, Matt and his father took her out for a birthday lunch. During lunch, Matt's father reached over and took Katie's hand. He told her that Matt and he had spoken, and he wanted her to know that he would be so honored at the prospect of having Katie as his daughter-in-law one day. Katie's guards began to lower more. The very next day, Matt disappeared again. No matter how many times Katie called, emailed, or texted, he wouldn't respond. She called Matt's friends; no one had seen him. She called his family, and they told her they didn't want to get involved. After a month of this, Katie decided to drive to Matt's house and confront him. When she arrived, something felt amiss, putting Katie right back into the mode of high alert that she had been in her entire childhood around her mother. As she inquired where Matt had been, he told her that he didn't know if anything he ever felt for her was real. He didn't want to be with her anymore. He didn't think he ever loved her. He never wanted to talk to her again. Katie's head began swirling and she couldn't breathe. She didn't believe what she was hearing, and begged him to stop acting this way and saying these things. Matt looked her in the eyes and said "I'm done. Get out." It was the last time Katie ever saw or spoke to Matt.

What we see from Katie's story is that in this manifestation, she chose to get over the Core Karmic lesson of self-worth, and fear of abandonment was the main symptom lesson of her lack of self-worth. She chose both parents, step-parent, and grandparent to show her the lesson, and grew up in a difficult situation that caused a lot of Karmic lessons to pop up. Before meeting her first non-family Karmic – Matt – Katie was developing patterns that were very specifically pointing to what she needed to heal.

The lesson that Katie did learn from Matt was that of not abandoning others for fear of being abandoned. Though this was not the full expression and purpose of the Karmic relationship, the remainder of her and Matt's relationship was just retriggering Katie to the point of detriment as opposed to grasping the situation. At that point, the Higher Self came in and cut it off, causing a major affliction of the same Karmic lesson that Katie was refusing to learn.

With Karmics, the recurrence of patterns ultimately get so obvious that they will grant the capability to look back and recognize them in correlation to understanding the purpose of the Soul Family members and Core Karmic lesson. The ability for Katie to recognize I AM allocates the skill to comprehend that one can never be truly abandoned, even if programmed to egoically abandon the Self.

When Karmic relationships are cut off by the Higher Self, they're generally done so via the same lesson one needs to learn. It's the last showcase of the purpose you manifested the Karmic to present you. Unfortunately, this is usually what is happening when one's parent dies young. As stated previously, if one isolates themself from the world, there will usually be a permanent Karmic relationship that continuously makes them grow, and a very common one is children. This is also a common theme when a parent dies at a young age and the other is left to take care of the child(ren) alone. The parent that died is the Core Karmic lesson for the child(ren), whereas the parent who remains, is needing the child(ren) as their Karmic teachers. Instead of divorce, the universe steps in and cuts off the dynamic.

In another example, if the Core Karmic lesson is non-attachment, Karmic relationships may appear as those who continuously ask for, expect, or date/marry for money. Or they could appear as the opposite, where all of the Karmic relationships have money and are incredibly attached to it as well. But if it is not learned that money is fleeting, the Higher Self will step in and make it very apparent via things like stock market crashes; high alimony payments; loss of job; loss of possessions; loss of security; partners leaving for more wealthy partners; partners leaving for love instead of money; the list goes on.

All Karmic relationships are meant to show you the same Core Karmic lesson and symptom Karmic lessons. However, certain Karmics also come into your life in order to teach you smaller lessons, and I call these *Small Karmics*. These are the Karmic relationships that tend to lead you towards other members of your Soul Family, and they are generally the ones that tend to fade away as opposed to the universe ending them. Nevertheless, it's not uncommon to stay in a relationship with a Small Karmic due to egoic pressures and expectations.

For example, you may not view omission as a lie, believing that if you just omit something, or if it does not come up, you're technically not lying. A Small Karmic may omit something to you that is pertinent information in order for you to make your own decision about the situation. Once you find out that they omitted, you feel betrayed and that they manipulated you. Although you forgive them for the omission, once you, yourself begin to be upfront about things and not omit, you have learned the lesson. You may at that point have no want or desire for the Small Karmic to be in your life anymore, yet you remain in the situation. But what happens when you stay in the situation instead of letting it naturally fade away, is that the 5D energy will continuously show you the same lesson again, and again, and again, even though you already learned it. You are at this point pushing against universal energy of flow and expansion, and will finally get so angry, agitated, annoyed, or apathetic, that you will end the relationship, either directly or indirectly. In certain lifetimes, you will also actively end the familial Karmic relationship.

The other Small Karmics that are common, are teachers when we were younger. A question I get asked all the time is whether someone's teacher when they were in elementary school or high school was a Soulmate. This teacher pushed them to go to X college or put them on a path of what their job ended up becoming as an adult or made them feel safe when their home environment wasn't so. These people were not Soulmates, they were Small Karmics. They directed you to the correct path of where the Higher Self wanted to go in order for this Ego to learn the most lessons that it could as an adult. As much as this teacher meant to you and as much as you've built them up in your head to be one of the most influential people in your youth, let this be a realization that Karmics are a very important part of the Soul Family, and they are all appreciated.

Karmics are what are referred to as "toxic people"

There will come a point during your Karmic relationship where you will absolutely feel with every bit of your being "I am done," especially when the Karmic relationship is that of an intimate nature. There is also a point in which you may feel absolutely disgusted by your Karmic, and everything in you will be screaming to end the relationship and never return to it. After all, there is no one who can cause anger like a Karmic.

Karmic relationships are incredibly tumultuous. It's what your friends would label as a "toxic relationship," or your Karmic as a "toxic person." If you've ever been in an abusive relationship, that was a Karmic relationship or lesson at play. The same goes for any relationship where afterward the person stalked, spoke ill about you, or defamed your character, and vice versa. A beautiful part of Karmic relationships, though, is that when you have learned the lessons needed, the attachment to the Karmic will lessen, even when you're still in the relationship.

If it hasn't faded yet, you still have not learned the lesson they were meant to teach you.

Please note: if you are currently in an abusive relationship, especially physical, please seek help. Just because it is a Karmic relationship or lesson DOES NOT mean that it's okay in any way, shape, or form!

Phoebe's story

Phoebe had dealt with bouts of depression her entire life and felt like no one understood her. She was a cutter and numbed the rest of her pain with drugs. Phoebe met Adam through a mutual friend when she was sixteen years old, and he was the first person she encountered who seemed to have as bleak of an outlook on life as she did. They were immediately drawn to one another, and dated for a brief time until Phoebe's parents forbade her from seeing him. During the time that they dated, Adam was living in his car or crashing on friends' couches, with Phoebe calling him each morning to make sure he was eating, applying for jobs, and not slipping too far into depression.

When Phoebe was eighteen, Adam reached out to her and they began a friendship; Adam always pushing for more, and Phoebe too depressed and too strung out on drugs to care. Adam would physically go to Phoebe's house, get her out of bed, dress her, and make sure she functioned for the day without hurting herself. He was helping her just as she had helped him. But after two months of doing this daily, Adam said "enough," and cut off communication.

Over the course of the next seven years, Phoebe and Adam would randomly and consistently run into each other. In as large of a city as they lived in, Phoebe found it strange, but Adam didn't seem to notice. During this time, Adam had started dating a girl whom he ultimately married. Phoebe had gotten clean from drugs, finished college, and traveled Europe. Though things looked great externally, when Phoebe was twenty-five years old, she had a major depressive episode that landed her in hospital. For six months she battled herself, lost herself, and lost trust in herself and her ability to make even the most basic of decisions. When she finally came out of her delirium, Phoebe wanted to change her life and opened a store selling crystals and mysticism paraphernalia. Though she was much more contented living this life, she was absolutely terrified of falling back down the well of darkness she had just pulled herself out of, and she still had residual trouble trusting herself in making basic decisions. Phoebe gave all decision making control – even over her own life – to whomever was around her.

Six months after opening her store, Adam wandered in. They were both flabbergasted at running into each other again, and they made plans to get lunch. Later that week, Adam told Phoebe that he was currently going through a divorce. Phoebe began adamantly pursuing Adam. She believed that he was the only person who had ever understood her and that he'd be safe because she had known him for so long. She would help him through his divorce as he would help her through her mental recovery.

But life wasn't so rosy with Adam. His divorce made him bitter towards women, jealous, possessive, paranoid, and mean. He made Phoebe end all relationships with her male friends due to jealousy. Except for work, Adam wouldn't let Phoebe leave the house without him in case she ran into a guy she ended up liking more than him. He told Phoebe how to dress so she wasn't "trying so hard," and yelled at her if she put on makeup; "Who are you trying to impress at your work!?" was a constant accusation. He told Phoebe what to eat; what to cook; where she could go; what she could do; when she could talk to her friends; and who she could talk to in general. On top of all of it, Adam quit his job and moved into Phoebe's house to "keep an eye on her." If Phoebe ever tried to stand up for herself, Adam would gaslight her and tell her she was "crazy;" a phrase that was exceedingly scary to Phoebe since she had just been through a breakdown. So Phoebe let Adam steamroll her because she believed she could not trust herself.

Then came the day that Adam began to get physically violent. It began with small motions, like holding Phoebe's arms behind her back and yelling in her face when she tried to disagree with him; slamming her into walls; and telling her it was her "duty" as his partner to take care of his sexual needs whenever he wanted, even after he had physically assaulted her. Each time after Adam's abuse, he would break down into tears and make Phoebe hold him as he sobbed that she was "making him do these things." It was Phoebe's fault; it was Phoebe who was "forcing" him to act out due to her lack of mental stability that he had seen since she was sixteen. Phoebe believed him.

On one particular day, Adam was on a tirade and threw Phoebe to the ground. He got on top of her, held her throat, and punched the ground next to her face, breaking his hand on the concrete floor under the carpet. As Phoebe drove Adam to hospital, he screamed about how she made him punch the ground. *Why was she so crazy?* He kept asking. At hospital, Adam did not let up; hollering in the hallways all the way to the exam room about how it was his girlfriend's fault that he broke his hand. A nurse walked up to Phoebe and asked her if she was okay. Phoebe didn't understand the question. The nurse reiterated the question and added that if Phoebe was in danger, the nurse would call the authorities. It was at this point that Phoebe began to realize she may not have been the culprit of all the abuse, after all.

The next time Phoebe met with her best friend, she opened up and told her about what had been going on with Adam. Her best friend – who knew Adam – responded that she, herself had never seen a mean side of him before, and therefore didn't believe what Phoebe was telling her. She convinced Phoebe that it was again, in her head, and that she was overreacting. The reply crushed Phoebe, and she again, thought the problem must lie within herself.

The abuse with Adam continued for the next six months. Phoebe began going to group therapy and private therapy sessions, taking antidepressants, antipsychotics, antianxiety medication, and mood stabilizers. Adam was thrilled at all of this and didn't miss a beat to tell her to "take her meds" when he would fly off the handle. Phoebe was being gaslighted by everyone around her, and held everything in, in fear. Adam began talking about marriage, and when Phoebe wouldn't respond, more fights would ensue. Adam drove them to a ring store and told Phoebe to pick one out. She didn't want to, but after seeing the look in Adam's eye, she caved. Since Adam didn't have a job, Phoebe paid for the ring.

The hollow pit in Phoebe's stomach kept growing in size, and the thought of being legally stuck with Adam for the rest of her life was enough for Phoebe to consider suicide. She thought she had hit rock bottom during her breakdown, but this was a whole new level of fear and despair. During her breakdown, her body was functioning off of pure survival, and she found herself feeling the same way now. And then Phoebe realized something: this was a *choice*. Staying with Adam, though she believed she was stuck in her situation, was still a choice. Her breakdown had not been a choice; it had been thrust upon her and she had made it through. But *choosing* this life and sticking with it was something she could no longer bear. So when Adam got down on one knee and put the ring on Phoebe's finger that she had purchased for herself, she stood up straight, looked him dead in the eyes, and said "No." Adam threatened to leave her, threatened to leave town, threatened to end his own life. And Phoebe stood tall and kept rejecting him. Adam packed his bags and left a week later.

Phoebe believed that she was broken and unable to make "good" decisions for herself. She allowed everyone to gaslight her even though she felt terrible about the situation she was in. When Phoebe realized that the very thing keeping her in the relationship – her inability to make choices – was already being practiced by *not making a choice*, she learned the Karmic lesson Adam was showing her. Adam had appeared in Phoebe's life at every moment that she needed to make a choice for herself, and take care of herself, yet it took a decade after meeting Adam for Phoebe to realize what the Karmic lesson was. The ending of their relationship seems like an abrupt cut-off that is told just to quickly end the story. But after Phoebe learned her Karmic lesson, there was no need for Adam to fight for or with her anymore. Energetically, he recognized that what had transpired between them would no longer be the case, even if he wasn't mentally aware of it. So he packed his bags and left. Karmic relationships unfortunately don't always end as easily as this one, but surprisingly, the majority of the time they do.

It's easy to pinpoint the lesson these "toxic" relationships were meant to teach us. The relationship ends with us saying "I will NEVER put myself in that situation EVER again." Karmics can bring out the absolute worst in us and vice versa, but that's technically the point; to change this thing about ourself.

However, there is no such thing as a toxic person or a toxic relationship; it's about perspective. What one person deems as "toxic," another person deems as "trauma." What one has tolerance for, another has none. To you, someone being emotionally unavailable and showing it to you repeatedly may look "toxic," but you have manifested this person to teach you a lesson, and you are making the choice to stay in the situation. You are creating the "toxic" pattern that you are judging. So instead, see what you're meant to learn from it.

When you meet a Karmic, you will either be immediately drawn to them or repulsed by them. Generally, it's drawn to, but if you've met someone in the past whom you disliked for no reason at first, only to enter into some form of relationship and realize you were right from the get-go, these are Karmic relationships. Small Karmics don't hold the same weight, but you might be intrigued by them, which ultimately pulls you in. The reason we're magnetically drawn to our Karmics is because without the strong emotional and energetic pull, we'd never allow these people into our lives. The same goes for Karmics with whom you're repelled by; the feeling and energy are so *negatively* strong, that it makes you wonder why you feel this way, so the Ego seeks to dispel the energetic theory.

Getting into an intimate relationship with a Karmic poses a lot of confusing emotions, especially at the beginning. Karmics can be very much the same as us on the surface: same beliefs, same ideals, same desires, same likes and dislikes, same personality traits. Or they can be completely different, leading to the phrase 'opposites attract.' The sexual attraction is usually incredibly high as well, making you feel like you have met the ideal person, or your "Soulmate" in the traditional sense of the word. It is not uncommon to feel physically addicted to a Karmic, both in the relationship and out of it. This leads to the notion that when a Karmic begins to trigger you, they can appear to be a Twin Flame on the surface. This is simply the Higher Self keeping you in the relationship in order to learn the Karmic lesson. This is, in fact, the entire sense as to why Karmics mimic higher vibrational Soul Family members. Though when you heal the wound or learn a lesson from a Karmic, your attachment to them will begin to fade.

It is in this point that we need to pay strict attention, for the egoic attachment to a Karmic is much different than an energetic one. It is with the Ego that we allow ourselves to be pulled back over and over again into the same Karmic relationship with the same Karmic partner. We felt that strong energetic pull at the beginning, increased it with emotional attachment, and have now egoically convinced ourself that it is "meant to be," when in fact, we are solely hanging on so we do not have to go through the pain of learning the lesson. Once the actual Karmic lesson is learned, you will not want to be with your Karmic. That's a promise.

Karmic relationships will lead you to the rest of your Soul Family

A magical aspect of Karmic relationships is that they lead us to the rest of our Soul Family. It is only after we've learned certain lessons that we are able to raise our vibrational frequency enough to find other Soul Family members. If we have been dealing with Karmic after Karmic and still have not learned the lesson, I AM will generally place a Soulmate on our path to aid us in getting through.

Nathaniel's story

Nathaniel had lived in the same town his entire life, always dreaming of exploring elsewhere. He was so hopeful of one day leaving, that he had saved quite a large amount of money to be able to do so. He was stuck in a menial job waiting tables at a diner filled with regular locals; the only girls in the town he had gone to high school with; and his friends were doing the same things they had been doing since they were all kids together. However, Nathaniel's entire life as he knew it was in his hometown, and he was paralyzed to leave when push came to shove.

A new busboy named Steven started at Nathaniel's work one day. Nathaniel had never seen Steven before, and he seemed *different*. Nathaniel was drawn to him. They began talking on their lunch breaks, and Steven explained how he grew up in an army family, and was used to moving around a lot; as an adult, he tended to do the same thing, picking up odd jobs here and there to support his nomadic ways. Steven shared his many 'tales from the road,' and Nathaniel couldn't get enough. They became fast friends, and Nathaniel looked up to Steven. They started daydreaming about traveling together, moving to new destinations and living wherever their experiences took them.

All of Steven's stories ended with "...you'll see when we go." Nathaniel began to envision his life away from his hometown more than he ever had before, and was anxious to get his new life started. So Nathaniel and Steven set a date to leave.

The two of them frequented a bar a few towns over where Steven knew the bartender, Chloe. After the bar closed each night, Nathaniel, Steven, and Chloe would sit around, drink, and talk passionately about all the places they wanted to visit, and what they would do when they got there.

The date to leave quickly approached, and Nathaniel and Steven got ready to go. They would first go to the next state over, where Steven knew a bar owner who could set them up with a seasonal job and a place to stay until they figured out their next move. But a week before they left, a girl Steven had been seeing called to tell him she was pregnant. Nathaniel was crushed. All the months of planning down the drain just like that, so he washed his sorrow down with bourbon at Chloe's bar. After three days of Nathaniel repeatedly getting drunk and metaphorically sobbing to Chloe, she told him that she would leave with him. The seasonal bar job and apartment to stay in were still waiting for them in the next state, and since Nathaniel was too scared to travel alone, Chloe would participate. Just like that, four days later, they left together and Nathaniel finally left his hometown.

A little over a week into their new lives, Chloe got a phone call saying her mother had gotten into a car accident and was in hospital. Chloe assured Nathaniel she would be back, but she needed to go home. Nathaniel continued to work, not needing the money, but not knowing what else to do or where to go. He felt that same paralyzing fear he had when he was in his own hometown, except now he had no friends, no family, and no plan. He didn't want to go back home and admit defeat so soon, especially since he didn't know when he'd get the chance to leave again. He extended his job at the bar and waited for Chloe to return, but she never did.

Six months later, Nathaniel met a girl at the bar. She was the most mesmerizing thing he had ever seen, and it felt as if a magnet was pulling their eyes to each other's. Her name was Robin, and she was a hotel reviewer, as Nathaniel found out later that night while they spoke after the bar had closed. Robin was in town for her friend's bachelorette party, but was leaving the next morning. Nathaniel and Robin stayed up all night together talking and learning about each other, and Nathaniel was gutted that Robin both didn't live close by and was also never in one place for long. But Robin would be back in a month for her friend's wedding, and they agreed to keep in touch and see each other again when she was in town.

The next month was achingly difficult for Nathaniel. He had never met someone like Robin, and he was hooked. He felt like he had known her his entire life; like he had known her even *before* his life had started, and he wanted to be with her. He couldn't explain to himself what this feeling was, so he chalked it up to "love at first sight." When speaking on the phone, Robin agreed with Nathaniel's feelings, expressing her own deep emotions and the desire to spend more physical time together. When Robin returned for the wedding, her and Nathaniel were inseparable. Robin had extended her trip to spend more time with Nathaniel, but both dreaded having to part. On the final night together, Robin asked Nathaniel if he wanted to go with her.

For the next two years, Nathaniel and Robin did everything together: lived together, traveled together, and Nathaniel didn't have a life of his own aside from Robin's work schedule. They had been to so many places together, and the allure of "newness" began to lose its charm for Nathaniel. He had loved a lot of the cities and towns they had visited together – especially Philadelphia – but ultimately, Nathaniel was in Robin's town, her apartment, with her friends and family, and based his life off of where they were going next for Robin's job. Though it seemed on the outside like the perfect situation, Nathaniel became unhappy and so did Robin. Without having created his own life situations, Nathaniel became resentful of the fact that Robin was always "in control." Since Nathaniel was living for free based off of Robin's life, she became resentful that he wasn't decisive, ambitious, and self-sufficient enough. The arguments mounted and they emotionally drifted away from one another, but neither of them would take the step to end the relationship.

Finally, one weekend while in Philadelphia again, Nathaniel thought about how much he loved the city. The night before they were scheduled to leave, Nathaniel told Robin he wouldn't be going back with her. He felt like he "belonged" in Philadelphia, and he had enough money to start his life there on his own. He said Robin was always welcome and she was also welcome to move with him, but that he needed to find his own path and one that he chose for himself. Neither Nathaniel nor Robin regretted the time they shared together, and they still keep in touch to this day.

Nathaniel needed to learn Karmic lessons of self-sufficiency and decisiveness. He manifested Karmic relationships to come in and shake things up, each one propelling him into forward movement which brought him to other Soul Family members and simultaneously teaching him the lessons: Steven set the wheels in motion to leave, yet the universe came in and cut the relationship off. Steven led Nathaniel to Chloe. Chloe continued the propulsion, getting him to begin movement, yet Nathaniel was still stuck in fear mode to be self-sufficient with his desires. The universe came in and cut the relationship off. Chloe led Nathaniel to Robin. Robin was a Soulmate and gave Nathaniel everything he had desired and ultimately taught him his lessons to where Nathaniel finally took action. Robin led Nathaniel to Philadelphia, which became the place that he was able to concretely take self-responsibility.

Karmics will lead you to your other Soul Family members until you learn the Karmic lesson you're meant to learn from them. Because Karmics are generally so tumultuous or appear to create turbulent situations, there's no choice but to move forward instead of remaining stuck.

Signs of a Karmic relationship/Lessons

These are some major signs of Karmic Relationships that you will come across. This list doesn't mean these are the only signs, and you don't need to see every single sign in a category in order to have a Karmic Relationship. But take account of the people in your life – both past and present – and see if you can find a correlation or repeating themes. Then sit and write down how each of the people who fit into this category affected your life, how the relationship ended, and what you believe you learned from them. It doesn't matter what you taught them; this isn't about your Karmic, this is about *you* and figuring out what your Core Karmic Lesson is and how you've manifested people to show you. If you find that you have a list of Karmics who did not teach you anything, or that none of the patterns match, put them into a linear timeline and view how one led to another and what the circumstances were/are. Your lesson is in there somewhere, you're just not seeing it yet.

<u>Family</u>

- Whichever parent affected you the most is showing you your Core Karmic Lesson
- If you were adopted, your Core Karmic Lesson is within that dynamic
- If your parent died when you were young, your Core Karmic Lesson is within that dynamic
- If you're extraordinarily close to your family and feel like you had the "perfect" childhood, the Core Karmic Lesson is within that dynamic

- Any immediate family member that you consistently fought with, didn't get along with, or triggered you in a manner to which you are still affected as an adult
- Any family member with an addiction or medical issue which had you taking care of them and acting as the adult instead of as the child
- Also look to your siblings, grandparents, step-parents, and immediate family that you saw repeatedly while growing up to show you patterns that you feel you are still dealing with in each of your relationships with others

Intimate Relationships

- You will either be magnetized to the person or repulsed by them upon seeing them for the first time
- Continuous fighting after the "honeymoon period" of the relationship
- The feeling that they are a Soulmate or Twin Flame, even though the relationship is incredibly tumultuous
- Immense sexual attraction
- You bring out the worst in each other
- You have a feeling of being addicted to the person
- Any creation of addictive behaviors within the relationship, or an enabling of addictions
- They re-trigger the same thing over and over again within you
- They remind you of a parent/family member who

triggered you when you were little

- They follow the same patterns of an ex that you don't realize until after the "honeymoon period" is over
- You have reminiscent feelings of how you felt growing up when you're around them
- They are abusive, controlling, manipulative, gaslight you, or have victim mentality
- At some point in the relationship, you will have the thought of "I am done," along with hatred or disgust for them
- At some point in the relationship, you will stop caring what they think, do, say, or want
- You will crave closure at the end of the relationship on an egoic level
- You may feel angry or depressed all the time
- Your relationship cannot withstand any healing of individual lessons or wounds, because they are there to teach you that lesson, not support you in it
- Once you learn your lesson, the attraction fades
- The same signs as listed below in "Other Relationships"

Other Relationships

- You will either be magnetized to the person or repulsed by them upon seeing them for the first time
- Something about them reminds you of a parent or past partner/friend who triggered you, but you can't

put your finger on what it is

- You have a hard time saying "no" to them
- Any creation of addictive behaviors within the relationship, or an enabling of addictions
- They are a brief portion of your life that lead you to the larger manifestations of Soul Family (Small Karmic)
- They are consistently telling you what's best for you, and how you should act in certain situations without taking into consideration your viewpoints
- They steamroll you
- They label everything around you as "toxic"
- You feel "less than" when you're around them, or like you're constantly having to prove something
- You are frequently in fights, tiffs, or arguments

Karmic lessons can be mass lessons

Karmic lessons can also be on a grand scale. What easier way for I AM to knock out the same Karmic lesson to a large group of Egos at once, than by creating a devastating effect? The 1920's saw the majority of people turning towards attachment to money after WWI. The stock markets boomed, and everyone – even those who barely had anything – invested their life savings. Prohibition led to bootlegging, crime, murder. Sigmund Freud's work in 1920 to explain human destructiveness, and also his *structural theory* (id, ego, superego) was widely accepted by the public, yet instead of taking a deeper look internally, Americans continued to purchase and produce.

From 1925 to 1930, plows and farming equipment decimated 5 million acres of previously unfarmed land because everyone was doing so well monetarily, that consumerism rose. And then on October 24, 1929, the markets crashed. People lost everything: their houses, their farms, their jobs. They threw themselves out of windows on "Black Thursday." In 1931, the fields plowed for wheat created an overabundant crop, but no one could buy it because they had no money. The farmers couldn't recoup their costs, so in order to turn a profit, they plowed more land and filled it with more wheat instead of drought-resistant grasses. And still, people could not purchase because there was no money. All of that plowing led to a loss of fertile topsoil, which blew massive dust storms across the U.S., led to the vulnerability of drought, and made an inhospitable atmosphere for crops to grow. And then the rains stopped. A state of emergency lasted for eight years, in which 33% of people migrated to California in hopes of finding migrant work.

California was outnumbered people to jobs, and public concern rose due to the state's infrastructure being overtaxed. By the end of 1934, thirty-five million acres of farmland were ruined, and the topsoil of 100 million acres of farmland had blown away. President Franklin D. Roosevelt enacted the Taylor Grazing Act which reserved 140 million acres of land as federally protected lands; grazing and planting became monitored to encourage land rehabilitation and conservation; and the Civil Conservation Corps began planting trees and building reservoirs. Between 1933-1935, many programs and agencies were created in order to help those affected by the Dust Bowl: Emergency Relief Appropriation Act, Resettlement Administration, Farm Security Administration, Land Utilization Program, Drought Relief Service, and the Works Progress Administration, which employed more than 8.5 million people to build roads, bridges, airports, public parks, and buildings. To top it all off, in 1933, President Roosevelt "seized" all gold, making it illegal for individuals to own gold privately, thus nationalizing it. Forcing everyone who still had money to sell their gold back to the government for well under its "value" (known as the *Gold Standard*), Roosevelt then raised the value of gold in order to print more money and stimulate the economy.

During the course of the nineteen years from 1920-1939, the Karmic lesson of non-attachment to money was shown, reiterated again and again, and eventually, those who did not learn the lesson, were affected. Though politics and history have a way of repeating themselves to nauseum, the beautiful thing to come out of this period of "time" was the invention of more sustainable agricultural practices. However, we as egoic people, population, country, and consumers, are always on the precipice of this fine balancing act that can ultimately destroy everything that we've known. Isn't it better to learn what's needed and remember we are I AM in order to not be affected by our own actions?

Letting go of anger after Karmic relationships

One of the hardest parts of Karmic relationships is the anger felt after the relationship has ended. The reason for this is because the Ego gets involved and we have a tendency to make ourselves feel like crap about putting ourselves through the relationship. This is especially true if the Core Karmic lesson is self-love or self-worth. It is in this stage that it's very important to forgive yourself, because this is actually where the anger lies.

At the end of a Karmic relationship, you may be incredibly angry. The anger is not at the Karmic, but in actuality at yourself for wasting your own time; staying in the relationship for as long as you did; not ending it before they did even though you weren't invested anymore; allowing the person to treat you the way they did; opening yourself up to getting hurt; etc. Figure out what you're actually angry about. Forgiving yourself is imperative so that you can move forward and not get stuck. You manifested this Karmic relationship for a reason, and you should not put any undue stress on yourself for not having learned the lesson on a timeline which your Ego is stating is appropriate. Your Ego is the reason you had trouble learning the lesson in the first place, so listening to it in hindsight is futile. Give yourself a break and instead of being angry, try to figure out the lesson you were meant to learn. Then forgive yourself for any misdoings you played part in, in the relationship, and anything else you feel you need to forgive yourself for. This will help to imprint the lesson into your Ego so you can move to another lesson.

If you still feel resentment or anger, even years after the relationship has ended, you have not grasped the lesson, for without forgiveness of the self, it becomes almost impossible to learn, and allows the Ego to ingrain deeper the Core Karmic lesson. We see this a lot with parental figures, always utilizing our past to justify why we act the way we do now. But your Karmic relationships will continuously repeat until you've learned to forgive yourself, as all anger stems from the Ego alone. You are learning the lessons that *you chose* to learn in this incarnation.

Karmic relationships will bring about a strong desire for closure in the end, especially those of an intimate nature. This hunger for closure is actually a very telling sign that the relationship you just experienced was/is Karmic: Soulmate endings are a slow burn, in which things sort themselves throughout; Soul Tribes don't argue; Twin Flames are never over; and non-Soul Family members don't trigger enough to require closure. With Karmic relationships, you may have a feeling like there is "unfinished business" with them, and this is a reason we allow ourselves to get pulled back into the same relationship over and over again, whether it be with the same Karmic partner or a different one.

If the universe steps in and ends the relationship prior to you learning your lesson, there is more of an aptitude for the Ego to need closure. It is very difficult to receive closure from a Karmic in which the universe ended the relationship, because there cannot be closure on a lesson you have not mastered. It is your responsibility to shut the Ego up and move forward, careful to notice any patterns that emerge in the future, or "symptoms."

If you are the one to end the Karmic relationship due to having in fact understood the exercise, you will most likely notice the Karmic reaching out to you continuously and for long periods of time. This is your Higher Self's way of making sure the teaching has stuck and imprinted onto you, and the Ego has not brought you back into old ways of thinking and acting. Do not fall prisoner to your Ego wanting attention or thinking things may "be different" now with the Karmic...they aren't. Your Karmic lesson is over when beautiful things begin entering your life, and if you return to a person or lesson that you have already overpowered energetically, the universe will have something to say about it, and it won't be pretty.

Soulmates

"THE CONSTITUENTS"

The purpose of Soulmates

The term 'Soulmate' has a generally agreed upon social definition as someone who is a perfect match to your Soul. We hear about Soulmates in a romantic fashion, and are always looking for our Soulmate to spend our life with. However, the problem with Soulmates as socially defined, is that we are not whole without them, that there is only one other person who can be a perfect match for us, or that they are a separate soul other than "I." As I AM, we know this isn't true.

The actual definition of Soulmate through Merriam Webster, is "A person ideally suited to another as a close friend or romantic partner." This is more akin to what Soulmates truly are, but with caveats. Being "ideally suited to another" does not signify a perfect match, for what is ideally suited for your Ego today is different than a year from now when it has grown and changed.

When you meet or spend a bit of time with a Soulmate, there may be a sense of having 'known them forever,' or having 'known them in a past life.' A Soulmate is a recognition of the same energy between you and them which gets filtered through Ego and gives the sense of déja vu, deep connection, euphoria, or magnetism. This is why Soulmates should rather be called *Constituents*, for they are and have been recognized as the ingredients, essence, division, component, factor, and fraction of the same universal energy that you are. Although we are all the same, that small portion of energy which is recognized in the Soulmate is from a previous Egoic incarnation of the Higher Self, and in the same capacity as 'muscle memory', I AM begins to break through when encountering a Soulmate.

Soulmates can show themselves to you in a myriad of different forms. In fact, they're the only Soul Family members who can appear in any form to you *except* short-term relationships: family, friends, partners, bosses, co-workers, and even pets. If you've grown up with or had a multitude of pets in your life, but a specific one stands out to you – the one that changed you, and you grieved like no other when it transitioned – *that* was a Soulmate in pet form.

Soulmates arrive when you have established your Core Karmic lesson and have been shown by multiple Karmic relationships what needs to be overcome. Soulmates enter your life for one reason: to push you closer to or into Spiritual Awakening, or what I personally call *Ego Degradation*. This is done in two ways. The first is via aiding in learning Karmic lessons by standing with and walking with you through a large portion of this life. After all, sometimes to learn, a soft touch is needed instead of the tumultuousness of a Karmic. The second way is by showing you that there is more than just Ego, and this is done during and after the breakdown of it.

You will have many Soulmates in this life

Soulmates come into your life after you have been shown your Core Karmic lesson by multiple Karmic relationships. If you have met multiple Karmics in your life but have not learned any lessons (for example if you've chosen to have a very difficult childhood), I AM will manifest a Soulmate to help guide you more sensitively. Soulmates also come in when one relies too heavily on the Ego and becomes stuck in Egoic patterns and habits.

Soulmates will be in your life for a prolonged period of time, but they *are not meant to be permanent fixtures* in your life. Generally, they last for two to twenty-five years dependent on how long you take to learn the lessons, and how quickly an Ego Degradation occurs. If you have a childhood friend with whom you're still friends with as an adult, chances are they are a Soulmate.

When you meet a Soulmate, there is a chance that one of you will not recognize the other immediately. But you will be in one another's lives, and the recognition of pure I AM energy will come quickly, leading to the feeling of magnetization. If the relationship is that of an intimate nature, the recognition will come faster and the magnetism will be immense. Soulmates, however, since able to appear in any form, will always make you feel insanely comfortable, understood, known, unjudged, and seen almost immediately. There will be a deep resonance between the two of you, and you will get to know each other's pasts, hopes, dreams, aspirations, motivations, and traumas. You will become, in other words, best friends.

It is not uncommon to have multiple Soulmates in your life simultaneously. If you are having a hard time learning certain Karmic lessons, plus have an added element of a turbulent childhood, many Soulmates may be in order for you to reach a higher plane energetically. If you look at those around you and feel intensely linked to many, these may all be Soulmates. You could be dating one, have two as close friends, have a familial member, and a pet as current incarnated Soulmates, and therefore may want to observe what they all have in common with regards to you and why you have such a large accumulation of Soulmates without having begun to break down the Ego.

Because Soulmates can make you feel like they are the only people who truly know and accept you, there is a propensity to date them. After all, if your Ego is telling you that you knew them in a past life, isn't it "meant to be?" Soulmates as intimate relationships are sturdy, dependable, trustworthy, overly caring, loving, and committed. Soulmates as intimate relationships are also entitled, needy, high maintenance, smothering, sensitive, and fussy. They are usually balancing two extreme sides of the same coin, which makes them overly emotional and egoic in their expression of care.

Though Soulmates can make wonderful partners that last a very long time, ultimately, you are hindering your growth by not allowing the Soulmate to push you into Ego Degradation. Being emotionally attached to a Soulmate and not wanting the partnership to end – especially if you're married or together romantically – hampers the ability to get to a higher vibrational frequency.

On the flipside, a large problem with Soulmates can be the strong desire to date the other, even if the other person is not interested romantically. A Soulmate may wait around *for years* for the other person, believing there is no one else that is better for them, or believing that they will never be able to find anyone like the Soulmate. While this may be true on some 3D level, it is important for each Soulmate to understand and realize the purpose of their manifestation. The "in love" feeling the Soulmate has for the other is just Ego, and if your and their Ego can acknowledge that the feeling is simply present because there's a recognition of singular energy in another form, hopefully, it will be easier to let go of the romantic attachment when it is unrequited.

The choice to be with a Soulmate romantically is commonly spoken about as a preferable option to being with a Twin Flame. Soulmates are stable, but they also do not spark your energy to expand on its own. Soulmates are here to trigger your Ego, for it is only the breaking down of the Ego that can propel one into Ego Degradation, and once this happens, the Soulmate will begin to slip away. This is why sometimes, during a "mid-life crisis," Soulmates who have been together for a long period of time may get divorced: one Soulmate has finally moved the other towards Ego Degradation (the "crisis"), and the two are no longer compatible vibrationally.

Soulmates have caretaker tendencies

One of the easiest and quickest ways of figuring out whether someone is a Soulmate versus another type of Soul Family connection is acknowledging whether one or both of you have caretaker tendencies with the other. This is especially true if one of you has abandonment as a symptom Karmic lesson to overcome in this manifestation.

Caretaking and co-dependency are unfairly judged as being inherently "wrong" or "bad." When one takes care of a child, do we view them as doing something incorrect? The innocence and inability for a child to take care of itself can be utilized as an equivalence to Soulmates: when one discovers that the Ego is merely perception and everything believed to be known has been a simple projection; when pure I AM energy notices the same pure I AM energy; when finally felt seen, understood, and unjudged; isn't this development innocent and worth protecting?

These caretaker tendencies may manifest as:

- Moving too fast, too quickly
- A lack of boundaries
- Prioritizing the Soulmate over everyone and everything else
- Anticipating the Soulmate's needs
- Feeling responsible for the Soulmate or thinking you know what's best for them

- The tendency to "people please" with the Soulmate
- Ignoring your own feelings and needs in lieu of their feelings and needs
- Defining your identity based on the Soulmate
- A hard time separating your feelings and needs from the Soulmate's
- Martyr or savior complex over the Soulmate
- Highly reactive to the Soulmate's actions, words, emotions, and feelings
- A hard time trusting the Soulmate but not letting go (this is seen especially in intimate Soulmate relationships if you've helped get them over an addiction)
- Minimizing problems within the Soulmate connection, or minimizing your own feelings and needs
- Afraid of anger, rejection, criticism, or failure in the relationship
- Passive-aggressivity
- High expectations of the Soulmate, sometimes bordering on perfectionism or impossible goals

There is only one way of breaking the caretaker bond with a Soulmate, and that is to push them or be pushed into Ego Degradation.

A large part of the caretaker portion of Soulmates is that they are the only Soul Family member who can get your Ego out of or over addiction. This of course adds to the co-dependency bond, as we can clearly see in twelve-step programs such as *Al-anon* or *CoDA*, geared completely towards those who have aided someone close to them get over an addiction. If you or someone close to you was an addict and either you helped them get over addiction or vice versa, this is a Soulmate. If the addict recovered for a while but dove back into it, this is not a Soulmate relationship, but a Karmic.

Anthony's story

Anthony grew up with parents in the entertainment industry. They were always busy on films or at fashion shows, running around, partying, or networking. Because of this, they introduced Anthony at a young age to all things debaucherous, including drugs and alcohol. By the time Anthony was eighteen, he was an opiate addict and had dappled in almost all drugs. His friends were also industry kids, so they either had the same habits as Anthony, had been in-and-out of rehab numerous times, or were too self-absorbed to care what Anthony was doing. But at nineteen years old, after Anthony dropped out of college, his parents cut him off and he no longer had the means to purchase prescription pain killers. Having no financial cushion anymore, Anthony's friends stopped inviting him out or wanting to see him. With his addiction and inability to get his hands on "safer" opiates, Anthony turned to heroin.

For the next decade, Anthony remained a heroin addict. He pawned any expensive things he had left over from his parents; dated girls who were also addicts; went from job-to-job just to get enough money to buy heroin; and lived on the streets at times so his money could go to drugs instead of rent. His mother had attempted to get him sober once, but Anthony's lack of desire to go through the tremendous pain of detox led him right back.

At thirty years old, Anthony decided to begin methadone and attempt to kick his drug habit. He also went on a dating app looking to occupy his time, which is where he became intrigued by Quinn. He told her he was on methadone and though she seemed hesitant about it, a month later, they began dating. Anthony felt intensely drawn to Quinn, believed he was in love, and 'knew' she was "the One." They moved in together soon after they started dating when Anthony got evicted from his apartment. Quinn was perpetually apprehensive about methadone, so in order to surprise her, Anthony began secretly dropping his dosage at an alarming rate. However, lowering the methadone so quickly stripped Anthony's body of opiates, and he began feeling symptoms of detox. So instead of driving to the methadone clinic every morning, he drove to pick up heroin instead.

For months, Quinn felt something was wrong with Anthony, but couldn't put her finger on it. Anthony gave her excuse after excuse as to why he was acting so strangely, but nothing appeased her gut feeling. Finally, Quinn uncovered that Anthony was back on heroin. She kicked him out of the apartment, and as Anthony begged for her to help him get clean, she refused.

Two months later, Anthony told Quinn that he was off drugs and did so without the use of methadone. He apologized profusely for everything he had put her through, and said he wanted to be with her. Quinn, however, had taken a job across the country and was moving. She told Anthony that she was elated for him that he was sober, and would love for him to visit her. A month later, Anthony showed up at Quinn's new residence and informed her that he had lied about being sober, but was here to do so and she was going to help. For the next two weeks, Quinn took care of Anthony as he detoxed: bringing him to hospital when he couldn't stop purging; getting him whatever he needed, and making things as comfortable as possible.

When Anthony finally came through, he told Quinn he was moving to be with her. She had "saved" him, he said. They were together for the next three years, and Anthony never went back to drugs. The relationship ultimately ended when Anthony began Ego Degradation and left Quinn.

Soulmates can be Karmic relationships

Though purely Karmic relationships cannot also be Soulmates, Soulmates can be Karmic relationships, and I call them Soulmate + Karmic. When a Soulmate appears that is meant to *show* you a Karmic lesson, not just help teach it to you, the mixture of the two occur. The best way of exemplifying this is via Quinn's story antipodal to Anthony's above.

Quinn's story

Quinn came from a family who had always gotten involved with addicts. She grew up around alcoholics and drug users, and by the age of eighteen, she was herself an addict, dated addicts and drug dealers, and befriended them as well. At twenty-four years old, one of her Soulmates, Sam, dislodged Quinn from her own addiction. Since then, Quinn had made it a point to stay as straight-laced as possible. Yet, she was still attracted to other addicts or previous addicts.

When Quinn saw Anthony online, she was magnetized to him. But when they met and he informed her that he was on methadone, she ignored the red flags and instead focused on this *feeling* that she had about having known him for a long time. For the first month that they spent getting to know each other, Quinn went back and forth between her brain telling her she shouldn't get involved, and this energetic pull she had towards Anthony. After seeing him continue his sobriety seemingly well, Quinn gave in and they began dating. When Anthony moved in with Quinn, she began feeling in her gut that something was wrong. No matter how many times she brought it up to Anthony, he would rebuff her questions and give her answers that were glaringly obvious as lies, but Quinn didn't want to look at the alternative. When she finally uncovered that Anthony was, in fact, doing heroin again, she felt utterly betrayed and resentful. Quinn kicked Anthony out and put her foot down regarding dating an addict, but the pull was so intense, that she held out hope that he would change.

When Quinn got offered a job across the country, she felt that the change in scenery would help aid her broken heart and get her over Anthony. But when Anthony called her and told her he had gotten himself clean, she couldn't help but feel hopeful again for the two of them. She invited him to come visit, and very much looked forward to seeing him again. However, when Anthony showed up at Quinn's door, having lied and now putting her in the position of having to help him detox, the resentment became utterly palpable. She knew from her own experiences how rough detoxing was, and Anthony had nowhere else to go, so Quinn grit her teeth and got him through it.

Quinn was angry and hurt, feeling fairly hopeless at her and Anthony's situation. The two weeks of taking care of him was beyond stressful and she kicked herself for allowing him to stay, but the pull to be of service was too strong. Then Anthony said he was moving to be with her. Quinn was still so furious and distrustful of Anthony that her brain was screaming at her to run, yet she had just put in all this effort, so she acquiesced. Quinn wanted to reap the emotional benefits that she had felt when her and Anthony had first met.

For the next three years, Quinn was constantly on high alert. She was always looking for warning signs that Anthony was back on drugs, and got overly hesitant at the smallest of things. When he left the house, Quinn mentally ran through all the ways Anthony could find drugs. When Anthony was on his phone, Quinn questioned whether he was texting dealers. When he was in the bathroom for too long, Quinn listened at the door to see if she could hear the sound of a lighter being struck. Anthony began cross-addicting with alcohol, and Quinn was in a perpetual state of care taking. But she felt like she couldn't leave: Anthony had no place to go and no one to rely on other than her. He spent money faster than he was making it, and had no backup in case of an emergency. Quinn felt like Anthony was her child, and she needed to protect him at all costs while simultaneously resenting him for it.

Though Quinn was co-dependent with Anthony, he was also such with her. They were best friends, and Anthony supported Quinn in all of her endeavors, hopes, dreams, wishes, achievements, and failures. He emotionally supported her, made her laugh, and they got along perfectly. Anthony participated in Quinn's family dynamics and Quinn knew Anthony's family well, who repeatedly told Anthony that Quinn was the best thing to happen to him. This made Quinn feel even more responsible for Anthony's wellbeing. Anthony listened and dialogued with Quinn about everything...*except* what she was feeling in regards to his past addictions and behavior. This bred even more resentment in Quinn, but she continued care-taking.

One day, Anthony began getting depressed. They had just gotten back from vacation and Anthony lost his job. Over the course of the next few weeks, Anthony's depression got more and more severe. He told Quinn he needed time alone, and moved his stuff into the spare room of their apartment.

Anthony isolated himself in there, drinking nonstop and keeping his distance from Quinn. His mood began going up and down, he would start random fights with Quinn when he would see her, and out of nowhere, Anthony told her he was moving out. Quinn was furious.

Over the course of the next month, Anthony packed up his belongings. He told Quinn he wanted to come back once he sorted out his head, but she adamantly refused. Anthony moved to a different state and spent the next four months in Ego Degradation. Quinn has never dated nor been attracted to another addict or ex-addict ever again.

Quinn and Anthony are Soulmates. Quinn got Anthony over his heroin addiction, and thrust him into Ego Degradation, breaking the caretaker bond. Although they are Soulmates, Anthony was also a Karmic relationship to Quinn, and just like in Karmic relationships, if one isn't learning their lesson, the Universe comes in and cuts the cord. However, subsequent to Anthony, Quinn never dated another addict again, and this is because when a Soulmate who is also a Karmic relationship comes in, they are the ones to *close out Karmic lessons.*

Quinn knew the lessons she was always meant to be learning from Anthony, but refused to learn them while together, instead focusing her attention on *teaching* Anthony his. In

Soulmate relationships, we may have the tendency to want to teach the Soulmate whatever Karmic lessons we believe they are meant to learn, because we think we know what's best for them. If their energy is our energy, isn't it reasonable to believe we "know" what that energy needs? But this is a large amount of control we are trying to exert over the situation, and one that doesn't turn out well generally, since it's coming from the Ego. The co-dependency exercised – especially when we get a Soulmate over addiction – makes us conclude that the Soulmate needs to be "mothered," and that we're solely responsible for doing so. However, the Ego does not know the lessons other Egos are meant to learn in this incarnation, regardless of whether they're part of the Soul Family or not.

Co-dependency with Soulmates happens in all Soulmate relationships, and the purpose of it is for the Higher Self to retain the Soulmate in our life until their purpose has been fulfilled. Once the caretaker tendencies have been fractured from Ego Degradation, it is the Soulmates' responsibilities to wean each other out, which can be exceedingly egoically difficult.

Soulmates are the most egoic of the Soul Family

Because Soulmates thrust us into Ego Degradation, it is only relevant that they do so by touching upon our Ego the most. If a Soulmate were to ask you why you love them, you'd be able to spout out a plethora of reasons, all pertaining to egoic constructs: 'I love that you're smart, creative, caring, ambitious, motivated, and driven. I love that you know me, that you take care of me, that you want what's best for me. I love that you're a good listener, that you make me laugh, that you're willing to go anywhere and do anything for me. You have great taste in music and movies, we have the same political/religious/social beliefs, you're the only one who gets me, and we have so many similarities.' Soulmates are the easiest of the Soul Family for both you and those around you to cognitively understand why they're in your life on the 3D plane: because you both just gel well together. So much so usually, that if your Soulmate is a gender that you are sexually attracted to, it's not uncommon for everyone around you to ask why you're not dating the Soulmate, since "you two are perfect for each other." And again, these egoic similarities plus the feeling that you've known the Soulmate forever, makes it impeccably easy to want to date them and think that it's "meant to be." But oh, how things will change once one or both of you go through Ego Degradation.

It is also possible that you come from the same type of background as one, or many of your Soulmates. For example, if your family comes from old money, one of your Soulmates may as well, and this is so you can be understood via this lens. If you have suffered racial inequality, at least one of your Soulmates will have also undergone the same biases and judgments so that again, you can be understood via this lens. If you moved to a new country when you were little and had to learn a new language and culture, you'll probably have a Soulmate who encountered the same. All of these things that we believe make us 'who we are,' but in reality are just titles that our Ego has put upon us, will be emulated by the Soulmates. These correlations may make one feel as if they are mirroring with the Soulmate, confusing them with a Twin Flame. However, the reason for the similarities between you and your Soulmate, is to help the Ego filter the energy and allow that energy to recognize itself in the other.

It is also with severe likelihood (especially if you do not come from the same background) that you will have most things topically in common with your Soulmates. You could have both gone to art school or are in the same line of business; you could both be foodies or aspiring wine connoisseurs; you could love hiking, surfing, or camping; be animal activists or minimalists; love critiquing old films or going to the opera; etc. You may have both loved to party together when you were younger but grew out of that phase alongside each other as you got older. You may love trying new things together like tap dancing, or archery, or Jiujitsu. You may be travel companions, experiencing new places together. You may have been friends since childhood, scrapbooking mood boards or playing with dolls. Whatever similarities you have that keep you linked on the surface, a Soulmate will always be there for you if you need anything.

Because Soulmates are the most egoic of the Soul Family, they will know and love your Ego more than anyone else. You will feel understood, seen, and accepted by the Soulmate, because at this stage, you are still functioning solely off of Ego. You will feel unjudged, and like you can tell them anything. Even though you are linked to all of your Soul Family on both the 5D and the 3D planes, you will very much experience your Soulmate on the 3D plane of perceived reality. And it is through this very sense that they will push you into Ego Degradation: by overloading your Ego until there is nothing left for it to do but begin to crumble.

Soulmates are the first to leave your life during Ego Degradation/Spiritual Awakening

Since Soulmates relate mainly via the Ego, when one begins to encounter Ego Degradation, it is pretty clear as to why, on the 3D plane, Soulmates would be the first Soul Family member to leave when the Ego starts to deteriorate. The stronger the Spiritual Awakening and the stronger the "symptoms" of it the more amount of Soulmates will leave your life, and the faster they will do so. Ego Degradation causes a massive shift in the energy field, and that shift will no longer be conducive to the enmeshment of Soulmates.

Ego Degradation makes it so that you and the Soulmate no longer resonate on the same energetic frequency as one another since it lifts your vibrations up higher than your Soulmate's. This is also what breaks the co-dependency bond. Though Soulmates will cling to one another even after one's Ego Degradation, the only thing keeping them linked anymore are memories of the past and past energetic feelings. It is also common at this point, to have multiple new Karmic relationships enter your life in order to teach you new lessons that you were unable to learn prior to your Ego Degradation.

Harriet's story

Harriet had encountered depression for the majority of her life, though was lucky enough to never have it debilitate her. She was always functioning, and utilized her drive to be in the music industry to feel better about herself. Harriet was always overextended: managing small musicians and traveling constantly; critiquing music for multiple magazines; and writing music as well. She had chosen a difficult path in the industry for a woman at the time, the majority of those around her in similar positions being men. Because of this, Harriet built up a tough exterior in order to fight off sexual propositions and advances, sniggering behind her back, and continuous comments about how she should "be the entertainment instead." Harriet was a workaholic, onerous, and always emotionally on guard.

Since Harriet was consistently working, networking, and traveling, she had a plethora of Soul Family members in her life who were consistently playing onto and adding to her egoic strains. Harriet started feeling the familiar symptoms of depression. She pushed them away as hard as she could, but began getting a pain in her chest that was so extreme, she ended up in hospital. After multiple tests, the doctors told her she was overly stressed. Her Soul Family members did not desist from piling on their own issues, going to Harriet for advice, venting their own problems, and persistently asking her about her work afflictions. The pain in Harriet's chest got worse and was beginning to affect her work: there were times that she was unable to breathe and couldn't go to meetings for the musicians she was representing, nor to shows to review them. She missed deadlines and had such a mental block that she could no longer write her own music. She was drowning and her depression started sucking her under. Harriet made the decision to take a break from everything. The musicians she represented ended their contracts with her, and the magazines she wrote for told her that if she took a break, she would lose her weekly reviews. But Harriet, for the first time, could not function normally, and she wasn't able to write anyway, so she accepted their ultimatums and cut everything out. When Harriet told her Soulmates what she had done, they escalated the situation: "How will you make money!?" "What will you do for a job!?" "Why can't you just keep one job!?" "You've worked so hard for this, why quit now!?" The questions piled up, and none of them understood that Harriet literally could not currently operate.

Harriet spent the next month sitting in her apartment dodging phone calls and trying to take care of herself, yet the depression was worsening. Then the calls stopped. No one was checking up on her, no one was wondering where she was, no one was reaching out. Though Harriet was grateful that she was being left alone, she felt like she didn't know who she was anymore, and she began slowly separating from her own sense of reality. For the next six months, Harriet dealt with a full Ego Degradation, and when she came out on the other end, she was a completely different person. She could no longer participate in the music scene with its sexism and politicalness. She could no longer manage musicians who treated her like garbage. She no longer cared about reviewing shows to try to prop up the Egos of the musicians and make the magazines money. She wanted nothing to do with the entire industry she had been in and worked so hard in.

After Harriet's Ego Degradation, her Soulmates either wouldn't speak to her, wouldn't return her phone calls, or actively judged and criticized her for leaving the music world. Over the next few years, all of Harriet's Soulmates faded out of her life. They were always there if need be, but Harriet and them had nothing in common anymore.

When one goes through full Ego Degradation, the Ego as we know it begins to shatter. We are no longer interested in the same things. Our beliefs and behavioral patterns alter. We go through a change both in the 3D and the 5D: new neuropathways light up in the brain as if we had gone through

Cognitive Behavioral Therapy, and we open ourselves up to the Higher Self and begin to understand I AM. Our tolerance for things lessens; our value system changes; our self-care and compassion escalate; our interests deteriorate and we recognize the falsity of duality. We literally strip away the false notions of our perceived reality and do not function how we used to.

Though Soulmates are meant to thrust us into this very occurrence, they absolutely hate it when it begins to happen, and try with all their might to stop it. Imagine how it must feel to have a best friend whom you've known very well for the last decade, only to have them be a completely different person overnight. If you are still living in your Ego, your friend is going to seem odd to you. You are not going to have anything in common with them anymore. Yesterday they loved getting blueberry pancakes with you on Sundays, and this week they're preaching to you about how those blueberries have a universal consciousness. You're going to think your friend went off the deep end, and when you realize that this best friend is no longer who you've called a friend for all this time, you're going to slowly fade away. So don't take it personally when your Soulmates fade out. In fact, take it as the biggest compliment you could receive: you have raised your vibrations, frequency, and energy so much, that the person who knew you best can no longer stand you.

You are not meant to walk the same path together forever

You have recognized a fraction of the same universal energy in your Soulmate as you are. But that universal energy, though the same, comes with a different Ego in this manifestation. That Ego has a different Core Karmic lesson than you do in this incarnation, and that Ego has its own path that it needs to follow in order for you, I AM, to recall the grandness of yourself on a mass scale. Therefore, once a part of the Higher Self breaks down the portion of Ego that is correlated to ignorance, it is time to split paths from the Soulmate in order to continue growth, expansion, and Ego Degradation.

You are not meant to walk the same path as your Soulmate for the duration of this incarnation. You are not meant to be with your Soulmate "forever" in this manifestation. Your Soulmate, just like the rest of your Soul Family, is designed to push you further ahead in your Spiritual growth, show you that there is more than just Ego, and then go along their way. And you, as *their* Soulmate, are directed to do the same.

When you force a Soulmate relationship to remain even when you know it's run its course, you hinder your own Spiritual growth by clinging to Ego. The Soulmate has shown us that the Ego is false, weak, and keeps us bound by perception. Why not honor that Soulmate and actually learn the lessons you manifested them to teach? The Ego of both parties may feel hurt via the termination of the Soulmate relationship, but that in itself is a lesson in non-attachment and self-love. Your Soulmate will always be there egoically if you ever need anything; after all, they have been in your life for a long period of time in a very deep way. They will not throw you to the wolves if their presence is needed. But after an Ego

Degradation, a Soulmate should solely function on a consciously 'need-by-need' basis as opposed to a regular fixture in this life. And you should behave the same for them; do you not want your Soulmate to learn, grow, and expand? Your consistent presence is truly an impediment after an Ego Degradation, either theirs or your own.

The tendency to cling to a Soulmate – especially when you're in an intimate relationship with them – is a hard bond to break, but ultimately, just like with Karmic relationships, if the clutch does not loosen, the Higher Self will come in and cut it off. Though the relinquishing of the relationship will be a longer and more drawn out process, conclusively, there will be no Egoic choice.

Throughout history, there have been famous Soulmates who have refused to let go of one another, and they have ultimately been the downfall of the other. Not to say that this will inevitably happen if you don't remove a Soulmate from your life, but generally when Soulmates refuse to learn the lessons and move forward on their path of Ego Degradation, more egoically perceived "negative" things begin to happen to the both of them. We can see this with people like Bonnie Parker and Clyde Barrow; Edith Beale and Little Edie Beale; Wanna Marchi and Stefania Nobile; Olympias and Alexander the Great; Kim Kardashian and Kanye West; Billy Bob Thornton and Angelina Jolie; and even within fictional stories such as *Romeo and Juliet*, *Tristan and Iseult*, and *Helen of Troy and Paris*.

Signs of a Soulmate

These are some major signs of Soulmates that you will come across. This list doesn't mean these are the only signs, but chances are you will feel almost every single one of these signs within the category. Take account of the people in your life – both past and present – and see if you can find a correlation or repeating themes. Then sit and write down how each of the people who fit into this category affected your life, how or if the relationship ended, what you believe they showed you in correlation with Karmic lessons, and more importantly, how they pushed you towards Ego Degradation, even in the smallest of ways. If you realize that you have Soulmates that you are holding onto, journal for a while on why it's so hard for you to let go and what they're still providing you with. The reasons will be one hundred percent Egoic, and that can support you in recognizing the true Egoic nature of Soulmates.

<u>Pets</u>

- A rescue pet that you were immediately drawn to and feel like you understand one another
- A pet that is deceased, that made you feel like you,

yourself, would perish at the mere thought of it not being on the 3D plane with you
- A pet that is still alive that you cannot even fathom what you will do or how you will survive when they transition
- A pet from childhood that was consistently attentive and around whenever you were going through a hard time, giving you the feeling that you were not alone
- A pet that you are overly care-taking towards, to an unhealthy extreme, in which you completely alter your life for the sake of their comfort
- If you had a pet as a child that you felt any of the above feelings about, and that pet was given away, that is your Higher Self cutting off the relationship for you. Take note as to what was occurring in your life around that period

Family

- Any family member that has always supported you, cheered for you, or was on your side no matter what
- Any family member that was overly care-taking, to the point of being a "helicopter parent"
- Any immediate family member with an addiction, that gave it up to better care for you
- Any family member that felt like a respite from the rest of your family
- Any family member that you are very similar to

- Any family member who has taught you how to function on the 3D plane in a "positive" manner
- Any family member who has given you your perspective on things that has "bettered" your life
- Any family member with whom you feel a sense of obligation towards
- Any family member that you've grown apart from as you've encountered some form of Ego Degradation, possibly to the point of no longer speaking, even though there wasn't a delineated moment of argument

Intimate Relationships

- Magnetized to the person upon meeting or seeing them for the first time
- A feeling of having "known them forever"
- A feeling of having "known them in a past life"
- A feeling of having found "The One"
- Thinking you found the perfect fairytale romance
- Caretaker tendencies or a form of co-dependency
- Strong similarities on the level of Ego
- A deep resonance and bond to the point of being best friends
- A feeling like you will be with them forever, whether that sounds appealing or not
- Addictions are resolved
- Support in all things 3D related: work, hobbies, goals,

dreams, past traumas, anger, upset, and desires
- Absolute comfort around them
- Prioritization of their needs above your own, always
- When boredom, regular irritation, or resentment of predictability begin to affect your mood, the Soulmate is pushing you into Ego Degradation
- When you begin to have passions that your Soulmate does not like that you have, they are pushing you into Ego Degradation

Other Relationships

- Magnetized to the person upon meeting or seeing them for the first time
- A feeling of having "known them forever"
- A feeling of having "known them in a past life"
- Caretaker tendencies or a form of co-dependency
- Strong similarities on the level of Ego
- A deep resonance and bond to the point of being best friends
- Addictions are resolved
- Support in all things 3D related: work, hobbies, goals, dreams, past traumas, anger, upset, and desires
- Absolute comfort around them
- Prioritization of them over anyone else
- A feeling of jealousy when someone or something threatens the bond
- Longing for an intimate relationship with the

Soulmate or waiting around for them to be with you or choose you (unrequited love)

- A boss with whom you feel a sense of obligation towards
- A childhood friend that you can't seem to let go of, even though the only reason you're still friends is due to the length of time having known them
- Long-time friendships that have slowly become one-sided
- An ex who has remained in your life throughout the years as purely a friend, with no strings attached
- A friend with whom you used to be very close, but now only speak to occasionally, yet you know they will always have your back, no matter what

Holding onto Soulmates

Soulmates have been in our lives for a long time. They've known us as we've gone through a lot of things, and have experienced a lot of things with us. They've been our best friends, and the thought of ending the relationship makes us feel queasy, because we feel, in a sense, like we're losing a part of ourselves. And that's partially true, since we recognize a portion of their energy as being the same as ours. But we also know that we can never lose any portion of ourself, because we are I AM, and as One, everything and everyone is "I."

If you've consciously gone through an Ego Degradation, your Soulmates will naturally drop off and out of your life. It's painful, difficult, and hard to understand for both parties. However, there are times in which the Ego fights back and does not want to let go of the Soulmate, so we battle both our 3D self and Higher Self in hopes of regaining what we once had with the Soulmate. It's important to recognize when this is happening, because with recognition can come understanding and acceptance.

Hypothetically, let's say that one of your Soulmates is designated as your best friend. As your vibrations rise, you begin wanting to learn to become a psychic Medium. Your Soulmate may begin making fun of you; or telling you consistently that they don't believe in Spirit; or they speak or act negatively about what you're learning, or try to de-bunk your beliefs. Their energy is feeling *threatened* by the loss of you, and it's getting filtered through their Ego as negativity and jealousy, since the Ego likes to misread and perceive situations in ways that aren't accurate. The propensity at this point may be to stop talking about your journey and compartmentalizing each aspect (the Soulmate vs. being a psychic Medium) as to not upset either side. But what's happening is a spiritual growth within you, and with this growth comes a step towards your Soulmate being on a different frequency than you, in the end leading them to exit your life.

Now let's say that you ultimately do have an Ego Degradation, and after you come through, you want to find comfort in the Soulmate. Although you two may see each other and speak with one another occasionally, things will never go back to the way they were prior to your Awakening. You're finding yourself more easily annoyed by their Egoic constructs. You're finding yourself exhausted after being around them or talking to them (this is a *major sign* that it's time to let go). You are no longer physically attracted to them if you were or are in an intimate relationship. All-in-all, when it comes down to it, you are only holding onto them because you have been through a lot together, even though you are no longer on the same page in any aspect. They are stuck in the world of the 3D, and you have seen beyond.

This happens quite frequently with childhood friends – in both sexes – but particularly men. As social constructs and boundaries make it more difficult for men than women to make friends as they get older, men tend to latch onto childhood friends even when these friendships not only don't serve them anymore, but end up being detrimental. It is not uncommon for men to even stay in the geographic location of where they grew up in order to continue being around their friend group. Chances are, these friends from childhood were predominantly Soulmates, yet the lack of societal acceptance of personal, emotional, and spiritual growth for men can keep them stuck in a perpetual pattern of disregarding their lessons in this incarnation. Generally, for these types of men to learn their lessons, the Higher Self will come in and create obstacles: a job far away; a partner they want to marry; unplanned pregnancies; etc.

As for women in this same boat, we see those who have their Core Karmic lesson of self-worth being the majority of those who keep childhood friends for life, and we see the caretaker tendencies towards their Soulmates exceedingly so. However, it is more common for these friends to drop off at some point as women choose partnerships, romance, children, family, travel, or work over their friends group.

Signs it's time to let go of a Soulmate

You will know that your time with your Soulmate has run its course when you encounter one, multiple, or all of these signs. This is by no means a full list, so add your own if you have more. Remember that your Soulmate was there for one reason and one reason only: to push you into Ego Degradation or vice versa. If you are encountering signs to let go, you as Soulmates have done your job. Retain gratitude both for their help and your ability to learn the lessons, write down what you've learned, and hold the knowledge that they will always be there for you if needed. It's time for you to move further down your path with higher frequency Soul Family members. After all, you manifested this for yourself. Aren't you excited to see what comes next?

- A long-time friendship that has slowly become one-sided
- When your Soulmate speaks or acts "negatively" about passions that you have that enrich or benefit your life, mental health, or well-being
- Boredom, irritation, or resentment towards the Soulmate (resentment is especially apparent in

intimate relationships with a Soulmate)

- When being around a Soulmate physically, mentally, or emotionally exhausts you
- When you no longer speak to a Soulmate on a regular basis, but keep them around "just in case"
- When you no longer have much in common with a Soulmate, but keep them around because they've been in your life "forever"
- When you deny or compartmentalize universal spiritual beliefs (not religion) because the Soulmate does not believe in them
- When you deny or keep Mysticism to yourself because the Soulmate looks down upon it or speaks negatively about it (i.e. clair senses, Divination, astrology, etc.)
- When you feel as if the Soulmate is consistently judging you and your actions
- When you no longer truly care what the Soulmate has going on in their life, become apathetic, or even better, equanimous
- When all of your ideas, philosophies, and beliefs are no longer in-line with your Soulmate's
- If the Soulmate tries to pull you back into the realm of the Ego by repeatedly reminding you of how you "used to be" when you two were close
- If the Soulmate tries to pull you back into the realm of the Ego by repeatedly telling you that they don't like the new version of you
- If being around your Soulmate is comfortable in its familiarity, but uncomfortable energetically (the best way to explain this would be by saying that something

just feels *off*)

When you no longer have any Soulmates left in this life, you have either learned the majority of the hardest lessons or understood your Core Karmic lesson to the point that you can begin healing. This is also true if you meet a Soulmate but do not develop co-dependent tendencies with them in any form. It is common for Soulmates to come in and out of your life after an Ego Degradation, but once you learn non-attachment, it won't matter to you if the relationship is continued. You can then function peacefully around a Soulmate helping to push them into Ego Degradation while remaining serene in your own mind.

The Soul Tribe

The purpose of the Soul Tribe

The phrase "Soul Tribe" is a tossed around term that the Spiritual community uses to describe any friendships with a deep connection. Soul Tribes are also said to lead the purpose of co-creating a collective energetic heightening within the world, and by having a similar goal and "life path" as the rest of your Soul Tribe members, you together ultimately bring about 5D revelations to the masses. This is completely wrong.

As we have learned over and over, universal consciousness and energy has no care about others' Egos on a deep level, for we are the same, and the Ego is just perception to be experienced individually in order to remember I AM. Unless the Ego of another is going to help bring about Ego Degradation for your Ego (as in a Soulmate relationship), a collective raising of energy only happens via mass Karmic lessons or by means of energetic frequency.

Each Soul Tribe member is at the *identical frequency* as you when you meet and interact with them, and they will enter your life in order to create support for you as you recall that you are I AM and navigate through your own egoic notions. Therefore, Soul Tribe members should be called *The Pillars*, for they are the colonnades of reinforcement, displaying different attributes of non-attachment on the quest to become completely One again with the cosmos.

Soul Tribe members only show up when you have stepped onto your path of Ego Degradation, and they will disappear anytime you deviate from that path. The Soul Tribe will be fickle in your life and there may be times when you ask yourself "Does this person even care about me? Do I even care about them?" But the answer is always a resounding "yes" and the absolute beauty of Soul Tribes is their ability to participate in and showcase non-attachment.

Soul Tribes will appear to you as friends only. They will not be your family members and they will not be romantic relationships. You may attempt to have a romantic relationship with a Soul Tribe member, yet it will not work: the chemistry will not be there, and something will just feel 'off.' The reason for this, is because Soul Tribes are not meant to teach you anything, and therefore, are of no benefit to the Higher Self in everyday relationships. If Soul Families in general are equated to a horse-drawn carriage bringing you from being spiritually asleep to Enlightenment, the Soul Tribe would merely be the bench you sit upon inside the carriage. You could easily sit on the saddle, ride bareback, or hitch a ride on a cart; but instead, the bench is a little more comfortable, and you can have a friend ride with you.

Soul Tribe members are the second most difficult Soul Family members to meet

Apart from the Twin Flame, Soul Tribe members (STM) are the most difficult Soul Family members to meet. This is because your Soul Tribe is at the exact same energetic vibration and frequency as you when they come into your life. In fact, you may meet a Soul Tribe member, but have not raised your frequency enough to actually connect with them. You'll continue on your path, and when your vibrations match theirs, they will return into your life and begin interacting with you.

What makes Soul Tribes fascinating, is that they are not intrinsically part of your Soul Family. They become part of your Soul Family through integration based upon frequencies. Because the STM must be at a perfect match to your energetic frequency, it is not uncommon for them to come in and out of your life. When you first connect with a member, chances are you will be close and spend a fair amount of time with them. It is during this time that your energies are linking in the 5D and the person becomes incorporated into your Soul Family.

As we are ever expanding and growing I AM energy, the STM do not tend to stick around as a Soulmate or Karmic does. Meaning, they will not be constant fixtures in your life, and it is with a high probability that your Soul Tribe member won't even live in the same area as you (or they will move away after a few years of knowing them). It is not unlikely for your Soul Tribe to be scattered across cities, states, or even countries. As they are meant to support you in the breaking down of specific

Egoic characteristics and reinforce practicing non-attachment, you can go years without speaking to your Soul Tribe, only to feel like no time has passed when you do have contact. You will also only have contact with the STM when they are specifically meant to aid in upholding their job within your life, based upon whatever pillar they are.

The Soul Tribe meets us on our identical frequency in order to bolster our ability to understand certain Egoic notions and help us practice non-attachment. The only way for the STM to be on the same wavelength as us is when we have entered the "correct" life path of remembering that we are the universe through Ego Degradation. Nothing extraordinary may be occurring around us that we perceive anything to be different, but even a slight shift in our mentality, memory, energetic pulse, actions, or subconscious musings can propel us into the right lane. After meeting a Soul Tribe member, we will be more prone to viewing our recent endeavors through a new lens, and observing how the Ego has, in fact, changed.

Due to these slight adjustments in frequencies, STM can be very difficult to hold onto, while simultaneously being the absolute easiest Soul Family members to keep. Again, as we are ever expanding, our vibrations are always changing. As a result, two things can happen with the Soul Tribe. The first, is that if you stray from your proper path, the Soul Tribe will disappear.

But as mentioned above, once your vibrations return to where they "should" be, the STM will return.

This is not to be confused with time spent apart from the Soul Tribe, for they are completely different things, and this is where it gets slightly confusing. There is a difference between losing a Soul Tribe member due to walking on the wrong path versus the normal non-attachment to them. The nuances are slight, but if you are discerning, you'll be able to tell the difference. Here are two examples:

Example 1: Sam has been friends with Abigail, whom she met in a group guided meditation. Abigail moves to another state, but her and Sam talk on the phone once a month about their meditation practice. Sam begins to get deeper into meditation: going on retreats, getting certified to teach, and starting a meditation podcast. She's so busy, that she hasn't spoken to Abigail in four months. When Sam has a moment to breathe, Abigail reaches out and they speak like no time has passed. There is no 'catching up,' no hostilities for not having spoken, and no stress. Sam and Abigail have simply been living their own paths, but still supporting one another from afar.

Example 2: Sam has been friends with Abigail, whom she met in a group guided meditation. Abigail moves to another state, but her and Sam talk on the phone once a month about their meditation practice. Sam meets Cory at a Yoga workshop, and begins dating him. Sam cancels her and Abigail's monthly phone conversation because she's going out of town for the weekend with Cory. Sam has abandoned her meditation practice, works more hours at her office job, and spends her free time with Cory. Sam and Cory date for eight months, but Cory is a Karmic relationship. Finally, they break up. Sam still doesn't return to her meditation practice, unable to find the motivation to do so. She continues getting into relationships with Karmics and Soulmates, and after three and a half years of doing so, finally learns her Karmic lessons and begins moving back into her Spiritual practice. One day out of the blue, Sam receives an e-mail from Abigail saying she'll be in town and would love to get coffee. They haven't spoken in almost four years. For the past four years, Abigail and Sam were no longer on the same frequency, and dropped out of each other's life. It is not until Sam reclaimed her true path that Abigail returned.

You will never fight with a Soul Tribe member. They are not like normal friendships or relationships where you have differences of opinion and go at one another. Instead, any differences that you have with the other, you utilize to catapult the Soul Family bond. Also, because Soul Tribes are fairly non-attached to you, there is less of a propensity to care about what they do, believe, think, or say. If you find that you are arguing with a Soul Tribe member, or getting truly upset by something they are doing, *they are not part of your Soul Tribe.* They are instead a Karmic, Soulmate, or non-Soul Family member. Your STM will genuinely want the best for you, and vice versa.

With this being said, you may also never feel fully comfortable with your STM. Because they're technically not part of your Soul Family until you incorporate them into it, there is not a deep bond and feeling of knowing them like there is with the other Soul Family members. You may at times feel intimidated, slightly guarded, 'less cool than,' more experienced, or further along on the spiritual path than they are. Your Soul Tribe will never know your deepest past experiences, stories, or traumas, because you will never connect with them on that level. They are not meant to give you advice or teach you through compassion or empathy of your past. They are meant to show you that there is loyalty and support for you, no matter who you are or where you came from.

Soul Tribes are split into five pillars

Soul Tribes are split into five pillars, each pillar a single person and representing a function of the Ego that needs to be broken down during the experience(s) of being a human incarnation. The five pillars are the *core functions* of how Ego and I AM symbiotically work together and create the vast illusion that is self. When you put them all together, you have a complete whole of the Egoic makeup of any human, and once they are each torn down, one can truly recall I AM. Remember, the Soul Tribe is not meant to teach you anything, but rather just support you in your own voyage through the mind and its destruction.

The five pillars are:

1. The pillar of healing
2. The pillar of expansion
3. The pillar of unity
4. The pillar of surrender
5. The pillar of continued awakening

You most likely will not meet the pillars in this order, and it is not a linear walkway through them. Meaning, you do not go from pillar one to pillar two, and so on. You can meet pillar four and then pillars one and two within a short time, and never meet the others. Or you can meet pillar five first and not meet another member for a decade. It's completely up to you and your frequency, who you've decided to manifest for what purpose, and what you feel you need support in, in your life. If you're stubborn and proud, you may not meet any STM. If you think you can solve everything and do everything alone, you may only meet one member in childhood. It all depends on how open and honest you are with yourself.

If you have less than five STM, that's absolutely fine; you have either not gotten onto the correct frequencies as the rest of them, or you have already learned certain attributes of Ego Degradation that carried over into this incarnation. If you have more than five STM, then you'll find that certain ones overlap as the same pillar. All this means is that you need a bit of extra support in this area.

Occasionally, a Soul Tribe member will switch out for another one. It's rare that this occurs, but that doesn't mean it never does. If you and your Soul Tribe member live truly far from one another, don't ever see each other, and have started only playing 'catch-up' and nothing else when you speak, there is a stronger probability that they will be replaced by someone closer to you in distance (or completely drop out if you have mastered the pillar they represent). Also, if you have gotten to a place with a Soul Tribe member where you think about them consistently but they are not reaching out to you, and you just don't 'have the time' or the motivation to contact them, your frequencies are probably off, and they will also most likely be replaced by someone whose vibrations energetically force you to keep in contact.

STM will never be friends with one another. In fact, it would be surprising if they've ever met another one of your Soul Tribe. A strange and beautiful thing about Soul Tribes, is that it's as if they don't actually exist to anyone except you. You're non-attached, they are there for you when you need them, others know about them, and yet, have never gone near them. You may introduce a Soul Tribe member to a Karmic, and *maybe* a Soulmate, but it'll only be once or twice, and they won't get along, or even remember each other. Unless you meet a member through a Karmic (and then chances are, the Karmic and Soul Tribe member will part ways), Soul Tribes are yours, and yours alone, and they should be kept that way; no need tainting them with others' Egos. STM are like forest nymphs that you must keep a secret in reality, and they only come out to play when summoned. Now, let's get into the members.

THE LOYALIST

The pillar of healing

You will usually meet The Loyalist right before you are betrayed. It's a possibility that you meet them directly after, but it's more likely to occur before, so that your energies can sync and you can energetically incorporate them into your Soul Family to support you when the betrayal happens.

The Loyalist is hard to spot until you've actually been betrayed, for they may externally appear completely different from what they represent as their pillar. For example, they may seem to be cold, aloof, detached, distant, crass, or completely into surface things and material possessions. However, the first time you encounter a betrayal after The Loyalist enters your life, you will immediately know that they are a Soul Tribe member, for their loyalty is so strong, unencumbered, deep, and solid, that it surprises you that a person like this even exists.

The Loyalist will always support you, no matter who is at fault within the betrayal. They will most likely ask you questions in regards to your situation as opposed to talking about themselves or giving unwarranted advice. If they find that you may have some form of Egoic fault within the betrayal, their questions will lead you down the path of making your own discoveries regarding how you could have handled things differently, or how your own actions may have catalyzed the situation. Regardless, they are always on your side.

As the pillar of healing, The Loyalist deeply supports you in your plight for navigating through Karmic lessons, such as fear of abandonment; emotional deprivation; feelings of entitlement; feelings of inadequacy; the demand to be perfect; the belief that your needs don't count; and feelings of unworthiness. Any childhood programming that has created Egoic trauma responses or symptom Karmic lessons, will help to be eliminated with The Loyalist as long as you are willing to do the internal work. The Loyalist is endeavoring to show you non-attachment to all things – also seen in their outer appearance – and if you allow them to ask their questions, let you vent, and still brace you even at your lowest, their unyielding support will assist you on your journey through the lessons.

Aside from incorporating them into your Soul Family, The Loyalist will only be present in your life when you have been betrayed, feel betrayed, or are about to be betrayed. If you are not encountering a betrayal of any type, The Loyalist may not respond to you reaching out to them, and you will not hear from them. If they reach out to you out of the blue, make sure to look around your life to see what is going on, if you have any feelings about something but don't know if it's true yet, or if you're being gaslighted. The Loyalist will remain in your life while you are licking your wounds from betrayal, and then magically disappear again when you can energetically handle it on your own. The Loyalist will completely vanish from your life when your Ego is no longer attached to the perception of betrayal from others, find true non-attachment to people, or when you have healed your Core Karmic lesson and can navigate through the impression of what others are "doing to you." Remember that betrayal is merely a perception, and it means different things for everyone.

Evan's story

Evan was an upcoming artist who was represented by an upscale gallery. He had his first solo exhibit quickly approaching, and he was both nervous and excited, for he had been trying to get a leg-up in the art world for over two decades, and finally felt like he was making it. Though his pieces were well-received, Evan believed the gallery he was currently signed with was out of his league as far as representation.

At the gallery opening, a well-dressed man approached Evan and asked to interview him for an established art magazine. The man's name was Erik. During their conversation, Evan felt a mixture of intimidation and energetic attraction to Erik. Erik was calm, collected, intelligent, and acted as if he couldn't care less whether he got the interview with Evan. But he also had a *je ne sais quoi* about him: elegant, interesting, and charming. As Evan told Erik about his artwork and his dive into the gallery experience, Evan couldn't help but wonder if Erik felt the same way about him. Evan repeatedly looked down at his own clothes, and paid increasingly more attention to his own mannerisms and the way he spoke, worried that he would put

Erik off. He didn't know why he was so self-conscious around Erik, but Evan desperately wanted Erik to like him. They finished the interview, and went their separate ways.

Ten days later, Evan received a phone call from his gallery. Though they had sold three-quarters of his show out, they were releasing him from his contract due to signing a new artist who was much more well-known than Evan, whose work was too similar. Evan begged to stay with them even as a group exhibitionist, but they refused. Evan was heart-broken.

Two hours later, Evan got another phone call, this time from Erik who wanted to fact-check a few things for his article. Evan told Erik that his gallery had just dropped him, and Erik immediately responded in Evan's favor. Erik said he was going to change the article to make Evan appear even better, and to call out the gallery for what they were doing, hopefully getting Evan better representation. Evan couldn't believe it. He didn't know why Erik was taking his side, nor why he would go out of his way to help him, but Evan appreciated it greatly, nonetheless. He asked if he could take Erik out for a drink as repayment.

The two met the next weekend and began to bond on a semi-personal level. Erik invited Evan to press previews for other exhibitions, and introduced him to other gallery managers. They became friends, though Evan realized he didn't know much about Erik, and vice versa. Either way, Erik was always there fighting in Evan's corner, and taking his side when a gallery, manager, or critic would rebuff him. Erik's loyalty to Evan was immense, and throughout the years of knowing each other, whenever Evan was betrayed in any aspect of his life, or felt that same sense of unworthiness he had during his first solo exhibition, he knew he could count on Erik to listen, step into action if needed, and advocate for Evan. Through it all, having a friend as devoted as Erik, who wanted nothing in return, made Evan start to truly comprehend that he had intrinsic value.

THE ALTERNATE IDENTITY

The pillar of expansion

You will usually meet The Alternate Identity right after a life transition, and your conversations will occur when you are feeling nostalgic about a previous part of your current manifestation. The Alternate Identity will be encapsulated in an Egoic life you thought you wanted, wished you had, or aspired to acquire. For example, if you grew up wanting to be a nutritionist but never became one, The Alternate Identity will probably be a nutritionist. If you always wanted to move to Italy and tried everything you could to get yourself there but it never panned out, The Alternate Identity will probably move to Italy, be from there, or have just moved from there.

The Alternate Identity will talk more about themselves than ask questions about you or than you speak about yourself. This is because they are painting a picture of what your life would have looked like, had you continued along the Egoic path that you originally desired or expected. Remember, though, that if you meet The Alternate Identity member and have a relationship with them, *then you are on the correct path for Ego Degradation*. Nevertheless, The Alternate Identity will always be supportive about your current path and where you're headed. They are your cheerleader, always.

You will be able to recognize the Alternate Identity via two ways. The first, is if you've just transitioned a part of your life, they will appear as having your old life. Over the course of knowing them, their life path will look almost identical to what you envisioned in your mind for yourself. The second way is that they will participate in and encourage whatever your new life path is, instead of getting excited about your old desired life. They may even completely gloss over, deny, or 'forget' that your old Egoic life path was the same as theirs. Or, in true Soul Tribe form, they may not even know about your old desires.

As the pillar of expansion, The Alternate Identity will aid you in finding acceptance with regards to your past not having come to fruition. The consistent stories, explanations, hardships, and outcomes they encounter and express to you, will allow you to live in a fictitious dreamscape for a while before recognizing that you no longer desire the same life you did previously. Your current manifestation is meant to expand and grow, not to be stuck in the past, and The Alternate Identity will exemplify this by consistently being on the move in some form.

Aside from incorporating them into your Soul Family, The Alternate Identity will only be around when you are feeling nostalgic or when you need someone to encourage your current life path (if the current life path is what's best for the Higher Self). Over the course of time, The Alternate Identity will become less and less available in your life, as you begin to appreciate and get comfortable on the path of expansion you're meant to be on. Because they are meant to help demonstrate growth, once you find acceptance of your true path and continuously expand on it, The Alternate Identity will most likely be the first Soul Tribe member to leave entirely.

Ryan's story

In the 1970's, Ryan had spent his entire youth dreaming of being a pilot. He was obsessed with everything aviation, and had in place a course of action that he would follow in order to make his dreams come true. As young boys do, Ryan would play with his friends, jumping off of things and running around, pretending to take his make-shift imaginary airplanes up and around the living room, backyard, and park. But the cumbersome cardboard box he utilized as his aircraft tripped him up one day, and he fell head-first into the coffee table, hitting his left eye in the process. Even though Ryan's vision was blurry for months and he wore corrective glasses, the doctor said he would make a full recovery. By the time Ryan was an adult, he was ready to begin his journey into aviation. However, upon taking his vision tests, Ryan was not only color blind, but had depth perception problems in his left eye, not able to properly align shapes together or gauge how far an object was. He was rejected from becoming any type of pilot.

Having never had another plan for what he wanted to do, Ryan went aimlessly from job-to-job. He struggled financially and didn't have any Egoic joy in his life until he met Mary. They dated for a while and eventually got married. Two years later, they had a son who had severe learning disabilities. As Ryan's son grew slightly older, he was not shown the proper care in school, labeled as "stupid" by the other kids, and too far behind in general learning, that the teachers wanted to hold him back multiple grades. Ryan's son had no friends, a strong lack of socialization skills, and was developmentally drowning. Ryan enrolled his son in a day program for other children with disabilities in order to help him socialize more and receive an education in a setting that was more conducive to his learning abilities. After six months of observing how the program affected his boy, Ryan was so impressed that he decided to apply for a Direct Support Professional position at the same program.

Two years later, Ryan was in the same boat as he always had been: he was happy with his marriage to Mary, he loved his son, and he was fine at his job. But he always had in the back of his mind the thought that his life would have been so much better if he had just been able to become a pilot: his family wouldn't struggle financially like they did, he would be able to travel the world, and he would be able to get the best care for his son. One day, one of the students' father's came in to pick him up. Ryan had worked with the student for over a year and had only ever met the boy's mother, but upon meeting this man, Ryan was somehow drawn to him. His name was Larry, and he was a pilot. In the brief conversation Ryan had with Larry, Larry told him that he was rarely in town at the right time to be able to pick his son up, which is why they'd never met before. Ryan immediately wanted to sit and talk to Larry, but Larry and his son left in a hurry, and Ryan didn't see him again for almost a year.

Upon their next meeting, Ryan and Larry had the ability to speak with each other for an hour. Larry told Ryan all about being a pilot, the freedom he had doing it, and how it was a "shame" that Ryan was never able to experience it for himself. The two men not only got along great, but Ryan was enamored with Larry and his life. Ryan invited Larry and his family over for dinner.

After dinner, Ryan and Larry spoke more about Larry's life as a pilot. Larry didn't seem too interested in Ryan's life, answering every question Ryan asked, and speaking for hours about his position as a pilot, his training, his previous time in the Air Force, and the places that he'd seen and been. These dinners became weekly rituals: the wives and kids playing inside, and Larry and Ryan speaking for hours about Larry's experiences. Though Ryan rarely spoke about himself, Larry always expressed how amazing Ryan's work was with the kids, and how great it was that he was able to be there for his son all the time. As time went on, Ryan became more and more jealous of Larry's position, and more complacent in his own life. One night at dinner, Larry informed Ryan that his family was moving across the country in order for him to join a new airline at a different hub. He would be taking his son out of the day program Ryan worked at, and his wife was dealing with re-integrating him into a new program in the city they were moving to. They would keep in touch, of course.

As the months passed, Ryan called Larry often and told him how his son was doing well in school, integrating better, and asked him about his own son. Larry's new airline had him on constant international flights and he was at home less than he had been prior. He sounded exhausted all the time and the phone calls got shorter and shorter until they ultimately stopped all together. During this time, Ryan began to enjoy his job more; feeling like he was really helping the kids he was working with and also incredibly grateful for the fact that he was able to be there for his son along the way. He thought about how his life would have been if he had become a pilot, and slowly began to become grateful for the fact that he hadn't been able to. The next time Ryan spoke with Larry, none of the envy for his life was there anymore, and Ryan felt internally sad for Larry. At forty-three years old, Ryan decided to go to college and get a degree in special education in order to be able to teach the kids that he had been taking care of for so many years. Larry fully dropped out of Ryan's life.

THE COUNTERPART

The pillar of unity

You will usually meet The Counterpart when you find yourself in a current situation in which you need a different perspective.

When we get tied up in the Ego and the emotions of Ego and cannot see a way out or any form of objectivity, The Counterpart is there to help us with observation for the highest benefit. They are the protectors in the Soul Tribe, and their main priority is that you do not put yourself in situations in which you can get hurt or repeat patterns that you should have already learned.

You and The Counterpart will be so absolutely and drastically different from one another on the 3D plane of Ego, that the two of you may wonder why you get along in the first place. Every Egoic belief you have, The Counterpart will have the opposite. You will never mimic each other in mood, feelings, or where you are in your current life paths. It is also not unlikely for you to physically look opposite from them.

The Counterpart is one of the easiest STM to spot, because they will be the person in your life with whom you consistently mentally come back to and say to yourself, 'Why?' *Why* am I friends with them? *Why* are they in my life? *Why* were we drawn to one another? *Why* have we not separated ways yet? But The Counterpart will always be there to grant you a different perspective on something you cannot see clearly through, or give ideas for something new to endeavor.

The Counterpart has the uncanny ability to always know when something has just happened to you, when you're going through a hard time, or when you need perspective or a jolt of creativity, even after not having spoken to you for a prolonged period of time. They will always be the one to reach out to you, and the aspects of their life that are going well, will be what are not going well in yours, and vice versa. Yours and The Counterpart's problems will be *opposite* from one another's. But no matter the differences, you will undoubtedly feel like you can tell The Counterpart anything without being judged, while knowing that they will give you an objective perspective to keep your Ego safe or remind you of lessons you should have already learned.

As the pillar of unity, The Counterpart shows you that duality is created in the mind, and we are all the same. The imposed opposite nature of you and The Counterpart exemplifies that even though things may look black and white, the actuality of I AM is everything in between and nothing simultaneously. No matter the costumes we each wear in this 3D incarnation, unity is the sole outcome, for there is only One.

Aside from incorporating them into your Soul Family, The Counterpart will be present in your life when something is going on in which your Ego needs a new perspective, or when your Ego is hampering your ability to energetically grow due to staunch ideas or beliefs. The Counterpart will also show up if you are rehashing old Karmic lessons and not remembering that you've already learned them. When you have become completely non-attached, or aware of the fictitious, Egoic nature of duality and begin looking at things through the lens of unity, The Counterpart will slowly fade from your life. However, as we can easily slip back into Ego when we are externally triggered, The Counterpart tends to be a Soul Tribe Member who is around for a large chunk of this incarnation.

Camilla's story

Camilla sat in a coffee shop in the middle of the day, blood running down her shin and cuts on the palms of her hands. She had been at a rally across the street, and had gotten pushed and shoved accidentally, falling and cutting herself on the pavement. She wiped the small pebbles away from her legs with a wad of bloody, wet napkins on the table next to her. As she looked around for clean napkins, a man stood in front of her and handed her one. Asking if she was all right, Camilla explained what had happened. The man responded that he had also been at the rally, and had seen the commotion. He helped her clean up, bought her a hot chocolate, and they ended up talking for over an hour. The man's name was Henry, and he and Camilla got along immediately. They finally set out on their own ways, and took down each other's numbers.

A week later, Camilla and Henry had dinner together. They didn't have anything in common except being activists, but funnily enough, they hadn't realized that they were activists on opposite sides. The rally that they had both attended were across the street from one another: pro on one side, con on the other, and Henry and Camilla were on opposing ends. Their political beliefs were so staunchly out of sync that they became very quiet, but after a few uncomfortable minutes, they both began laughing and continued their dinner.

Later at home, Camilla didn't understand why she was so drawn to Henry. She wasn't sexually attracted to him. She didn't have the same beliefs as him. She didn't want to date him, nor did they really have anything in common. But she liked being around him, and didn't want to end the new friendship just yet. Upon their next telephone conversation, Henry agreed.

Camilla and Henry began spending a lot of time together. They were never in the same mood, they liked opposite things, and they had completely different, strongly held beliefs. But the ease of being with one another was palpable, and they both laughed at the other and took each mood shift or surprised reaction in stride. One day, after having a few drinks together, Henry tried to kiss Camilla. She stopped him and informed him that she wasn't interested. He stated that he had been attracted to her since meeting her, and "maybe opposites do in fact attract," as the old adage goes. Camilla again rebuffed him, and he conceded, expressing to her that this would not damage their friendship. Camilla, having been in this situation before, was skeptical that their relationship could continue unharmed. However, over the course of the next few months, Henry had stuck to his word, and no difference was apparent.

Three months later, Henry began a new relationship with a woman who had the same interests as him. Two months after that, Camilla began a new relationship. Camilla and Henry still stayed in touch, though the amount of conversations became less and less frequent. A year later, Camilla called Henry to tell him that she was moving to a different state where her boyfriend just got offered a job. He was sad to see her leave, but said they would stay in touch.

Over the course of the next decade, Henry and Camilla lead their own lives: Henry got married, Camilla went through numerous relationships and jobs. Henry stopped being so aggressive about his activism while Camilla became more so. Henry would randomly reach out to Camilla, and to her surprise, it was always right as she was going through a hard time. They laughed about it when she told him, and always got along swimmingly when they would speak or see each other. But every time they hadn't spoken in a while, Camilla's mind would drift back to Henry, and the question of why they were still in contact. As she made new friends like herself, or dated a new guy that had the same core beliefs as she did, she felt like her and Henry were just holding onto a situation that wasn't offering anything to either of their lives. However, every single time Camilla became stuck in her beliefs or stubbornness, Henry would call her out of the blue and give her a different perspective on things. And every time they spoke, Camilla remembered why Henry was still in her life. They might not have been the best of friends on a daily basis, but Henry provided Camilla a respite from her own mind, and reminded her that just because she was so strict in her own opinions and beliefs, there was always another side, and someone there to remind her of it in a gentle way without any judgement.

THE OUTLIER

The pillar of surrender

The most confusing of the STM, The Outlier will most likely come into your life when you are going through a difficult time, but don't quite know it's a difficult time. As strange as this sounds, if you picture a prolonged period of stress in your life that you were unwilling to look at, The Outlier may show up and break down the barriers that you hid behind in order to show you that your current way of doing things may not be to the benefit of the Higher Self, or, that there are different ways of doing things that you were not able to see clearly.

The Outlier is complex due to their nature of appearing like the other STM. They may appear to be The Loyalist, The Alternate Identity, The Counterpart, or The Spiritualist at different points during your relationship with them, and this could leave you wondering whether they're in fact a Karmic, a Soulmate, or a Soul Tribe member. Either way, you are drawn to The Outlier and will be the closest to them out of the STM. Since they have the ability to present themselves as multiple members, The Outlier may be the member whom you reach out to the most when you are going through a crisis, or they may be the member with whom you consistently re-evaluate your relationship in order to figure out who they are within your Soul Family. They also have an uncanny ability to know what is going on with you without you having to say anything.

The simplest way of spotting The Outlier is via their attributes. The Outlier will have multiple characteristics of the other STM and vacillate between them: they can be spiritual one day and showing you your Egoic patterns the next. They can be the most undying loyalist this week, dropping everything to support you, but next week remind you of your old life and wounds. But just as the other STM, The Outlier will only be in your life if you are matching in energetic frequency to them.

The Outlier is the most 3D 'balanced' Soul Tribe member relationship, for you will both support one another equally, and it will be apparent how you are both doing this; a 'tit-for-tat' relationship, if you will. And just like the other STM, if either one of you veer off course, the relationship will be non-existent until you are simultaneously on the same frequency again.

As the pillar of surrender, The Outlier allows the Ego to remember that it is not separate from I AM, even during the most difficult of times. It is the universe's way of showcasing support, care, trust, love, and belief within a personified person to emphasize that you are All, and it is solely Ego that is keeping you trapped. The Outlier epitomizes all STM either simultaneously or through oscillation in order for you to recall that everything is created by *you* – I AM – and whatever you're struggling with can also be mended through you.

The Outlier will be present in your life more than any of the other STM, since they can exemplify all of the others in order to give you the best advice when you're unable to see through the fog. Continuous stress, lack of expansion, and free-floating anxiety is hard to pinpoint by the other members, for their pillars are exact to specific situations. However, The Outlier can allow you the space to feel unjudged and supported no matter the situation, and for this reason, they are the Soul Tribe member to remain in your life permanently in this incarnation, as long as you continue on the correct path of surrender. In your next incarnation, or the one after, or the one after, once you reach Enlightenment, you will no longer need The Outlier, as you will understand on every level, that they are simply a personification of yourself.

Amanda's story

Amanda rebound dated a man named Aaron on-and-off for years. Aaron was a nice guy, but Amanda could never get serious about him; they were just too different and Aaron actually annoyed Amanda the longer she was around him. Every time they parted ways, it was in a tumultuous-for-him and apathetic-for-her scenario. But Aaron's persistence and insistence pushed Amanda further away, especially when he would show up at inappropriate places, during inappropriate times to beg her to come back to him.

One day, Amanda ran into Aaron at a restaurant, and they spoke for a while. Aaron had just gotten out of a two-year long serious relationship, and had recently moved to Denver; he was in for the week visiting friends. Aaron seemed more emotionally stable now, so when Amanda received an e-mail from Aaron two weeks later telling her that she was welcome to visit him in Colorado, she perpetuated the conversation. In their correspondences back-and-forth over the next few weeks, Aaron continued to try to get Amanda to visit. He told her all the things they could do together in Denver, and wrote to her about his new roommate – a girl named Anabelle – that he believed Amanda would get along with. After another month of this, Amanda thought 'why not?' and booked a ticket.

Visiting Aaron was bittersweet. Amanda soon realized that Aaron had invited her there to guilt-trip and bombard her with stories about how she had crushed him the last time they ended things. Aaron was so persuasive and emotionally blackmailing, that Amanda gave in and hesitantly agreed to date him again.

One night, Amanda was smoking a cigarette on Aaron's porch when a drunk couple came up to her. Laughing, the drunk girl said, "You must be Amanda. I'm Anabelle, Aaron's roommate. I'll chat with you tomorrow, apparently we will get along *so well*." Anabelle laughed some more as her and the drunk man went inside, and although their first encounter was dripping with sarcasm and a bit of disdain, Amanda was interested. The next day, Aaron went to work and Amanda hung out at his house. At noon, Anabelle stumbled out of her bedroom and looked at Amanda sitting on the couch. "There's coffee on the counter," Amanda said. Anabelle stumbled into the kitchen and back out to the living room, plopping down on the couch next to Amanda. "So you're dating Aaron."

"I guess." Amanda responded, somewhat dejected.

Anabelle laughed. "Yeah, we're gonna get along just fine..."

For the rest of the time Amanda was in Denver, her and Anabelle were inseparable. When Amanda went home, she spoke to Anabelle on the phone every day. When Aaron went on a tour of Europe for a month, Amanda went back to Colorado and stayed with Anabelle. And when Anabelle called Amanda one day to inform her that Aaron had just gotten served divorce papers from his ex – unbeknownst to anyone that he had been married the entire time – Anabelle evicted Aaron on the principal of manipulating and lying to Amanda...the most loyalty Amanda had ever seen in another person. Amanda and Aaron never spoke again.

Over the next eight years, Amanda and Anabelle went through periods of not conversing for months at a time, to spending weeks together in person catching up. Whenever something negative happened for either of them, the other was the person they called to receive not only support, but also emboldening, non-judgement, or a different perspective. They were absolutely similar in past history, but vastly different in beliefs. They were loyal to a fault with one another, and did not encourage nor stoke the fires of any "negative" Egoic behavior, thought patterns, or actions of the other. Rather, they listened, and held the space for the other during tantrums, traumas, spiritual upheavals, and awakenings, when no one else would. They had been brought together by unlikely circumstances, but both made the other feel like they were never alone, even in their darkest times.

THE SPIRITUALIST

The pillar of continued awakening

You will usually meet The Spiritualist when you are already on your path of higher purpose, intensely focusing on spirituality, or after an Ego Degradation, and they will most likely walk with you through your spiritual teachings, learnings, or practices. For example, if your Ego Degradation has brought you to Yoga, you may meet The Spiritualist amongst those with whom you practice. You can also meet them out and about or in any fashion, but they will be easily recognizable since you will *solely* talk about spiritual philosophies or endeavors with them. Concurrently, you and The Spiritualist may both come from very strong Egoic backgrounds. The Spiritualist may be strongly intuitive, an Empath, or a Highly Sensitive Person (HSP).

The Spiritualist is the easiest Soul Tribe member to perceive, since again, they will be with you during your energetic recalibration towards the Higher Self and the 5D realm. The Spiritualist will feel like a respite from the rest of your Soul Family (including your Twin Flame) and non-Soul Family members, since they are *the only person/people* who will completely understand you on the 5D level. There is no 3D plane or Egoic discussions with The Spiritualist, and therefore they are experienced differently than everyone else. Because of this, they are *the most difficult Soul Tribe member to meet*, and stand for the most difficult pillar of the Soul Tribe; that of continued awakening.

You will have everything spiritual in common with The Spiritualist. The Higher Self is demonstrating that even though you recently went through an Ego Degradation, you are absolutely on your "right" and true path, bringing you others that will support you. The Spiritualist will not judge your Egoic experiences, degradation symptoms, or belief system in any form, but rather speak with you about them all and stand by you, whilst you move through. They will give you energetic perspectives you have not gotten to yet, or ones that you have or are currently realizing. Sometimes, they will seem more "out there" than you, or vice versa, and this is simply the Ego attempting to grapple with its new sublimation. Once you meet The Spiritualist, you have begun to truly take control of your thoughts, feelings, emotions, beliefs, and experiences.

> **Please note, The Spiritualist is different than someone who is religious, though the two are not necessarily unexclusive. If your Soul Tribe member is judging any facet of your spirituality, journey, or Ego Degradation, then they are not your Soul Tribe Member. STM remain non-attached, and therefore, have no need nor desire to judge, no matter their belief system.*

As the pillar of continued awakening, The Spiritualist is like the horse whisperer who can show the Ego what it needs to do without spooking it in the process. They will aid in your spiritual growth, spiritual understanding, and spiritual practices. They will let you know that you're not alone even though your energy and mind are going through a transition. And they will open you up to new things on the path of unearthliness so that you may further your expansion throughout your present incarnation.

Aside from incorporating them into your Soul Family, The Spiritualist will be present in your life when any large spiritual shift occurs, when your vibrations raise drastically, or any time you are experiencing Ego Degradation "symptoms." Once you are able to recognize and put into practice that you do not need anything external to accompany you in your Awakening process, The Spiritualist will begin to fade out of your life. However, the Ego has a way of pulling us back in at the snap of a finger, and so, The Spiritualist will be around whenever needed to remind you that you are All.

Cassandra's story

Cassandra had just gone through a lot in her life: the death of her mother, a breakup with her girlfriend, and a step-back in her career due to the stress of everything. She had, had an Ego Degradation, and now she felt alienated from her friends and unenthused about pretty much everything in her immediate life. She felt like she needed a big mental shift overall, and began reading articles on Astrology, Soul Families, and Ascension symptoms online. She joined online meditation classes and started following tarot readers on social media. However, all of the people in her life that she spoke to thought she was losing her mind and becoming a "hippie." The more her friends and co-workers pulled away from her, the further she went down the rabbit hole of spirituality.

Cassandra began following a woman on Instagram who posted daily mantras and musings on Higher Consciousness. Cassandra began looking forward every day to this woman's postings, and thought deeply about each and every one. One day, Cassandra was delighted to see that her self-proclaimed online Guru began following her back, and Cassandra decided to reach out to her and explain how this woman had helped her without even realizing it. The woman was named Zara. After corresponding bac and forth for a while, they realized they lived only thirty minutes away from one another, and decided that they would meet for tea. Cassandra was excited all week to meet Zara, but a bit worried that she would be viewed as 'spiritually inferior.' She decided that she would take the time they had together, and get whatever nuggets of information she could from Zara, without worrying what the future of their hypothetical friendship would hold. Upon meeting, Cassandra was amazed at how her and Zara spoke about spiritual things and she wasn't being judged for them. Their tea turned into a three hour endeavor, and Cassandra felt more fulfilled than she had in a long time. Zara seemed to feel the same, and she asked if Cassandra would like to come to her house for a group meditation class she led on the full moon. Cassandra accepted willingly.

Over the course of the next few weeks, Cassandra and Zara spoke fairly regularly, always about spirituality, divination, or astrology. She knew nothing about Zara's personal life or what had led her to becoming this spiritual, but realized that Zara knew nothing about her either. The next time they met, Cassandra began telling Zara a bit about her history, and though Zara smiled and nodded, she ultimately told Cassandra that though she found her journey important, she wasn't in fact interested in the surface level things that Cassandra used to hold so dear. She was more interested in what Cassandra was learning and experiencing *now*, after her Ego Degradation. And so their meetings and discussions continued, but always solely about spirituality or mysticism, never veering to the Egoic topics of society.

As time went by and Cassandra began reintegrating her Ego into the 3D plane of illusion, Zara would come in-and-out of her life, only insofar as Cassandra was having Ego Degradation symptoms or trying something new within the spiritual community. It was an unspoken pattern, and Cassandra never felt like Zara was judging her, but she knew that Zara would always be there when she felt alienated from those around her. Cassandra realized that Zara was not so much a "friend," but more a measuring stick to mark her own progression regarding Karmic lessons, continued awakening, and to understand her on a different plane and level than anyone else could.

Signs of Soul Tribe connections

These are some major signs that you have made a Soul Tribe connection. This list doesn't mean these are the only signs, but chances are you will feel almost every single one of these signs within the category. Take account of the people in your life – mostly present – and see if you can find a correlation. Then sit and write down how each of the people who fit into this category affect your life, and when they come in and out of your life. You will see that when you have left the path of what the pillar represents, the Soul Tribe Member will have also disappeared for a while. It's okay if you do not have a member for every pillar. It's also okay if you have more than one member for certain pillars. Journal on that and ask yourself what area of that pillar you truly need to work on, or what your past programming has made your Ego believe, to the point that you need more help in that one area.

The Loyalist

- Immediate, positive magnetism to them
- They entered your life right before you were betrayed by someone (possibly right after, but more likely before)
- If you met them without a betrayal in your path, the Loyalist did not integrate into your life until *right before you were betrayed*
- Their loyalty surprises you
- They are always on your side
- They ask questions instead of giving advice
- They ask questions in order to show you how you may have had fault in the situation
- They rarely talk about themselves unless specifically asked
- They live far away
- They seem aloof most of the time
- Their outward appearance sometimes intimidates your Ego
- They disappear from your life when everything is going well

The Alternate Identity

- Immediate, positive magnetism to them
- They entered your life during or directly after a large transition
- If you met them without a transition happening in your life, the Alternate Identity did not integrate into your life until *the transition occurred*
- They live the life you thought you would obtain/attain
- They talk nonstop about themselves
- They do not ask questions about your life unless you begin talking about yourself
- They do not give advice unless specifically asked
- They live far away
- They are gregarious and liked by most
- They are always busy
- They continuously cheerlead everything you're doing in your life
- They disappear from your life when you acknowledge that the path you're on is the correct one

The Counterpart

- Immediate, positive magnetism to them
- They are completely opposite to you in every single way, including (possibly) their physical appearance
- You have one main thing in common with them, but you may not have the same beliefs about that one thing
- When they are not present in your life, you wonder why you became friends

- You wonder why you two have remained friends when you are both so different
- You never judge one another for your opposing beliefs
- They are protective over you
- They freely give advice, even when not asked, but their advice is not judgmental
- They live far away
- You equally speak about your lives
- When the Counterpart's life is problematic in one area, yours is going well in that area or vice versa
- The relationship with them is playful
- The Counterpart will reach out randomly when you have just gone through something egoically powerful

The Outlier

- Immediate, positive magnetism to them
- One of your closest friends
- They entered your life when you were consumed with stress but didn't necessarily realize it
- They confuse you as to whether they are a Soulmate, Karmic, Soul Tribe Member, or non-Soul Family member
- You never judge one another
- They flip back and forth between STM
- They live far away
- They remind you of yourself egoically
- They remind you of another Soulmate you've had/ have
- You go back and forth with them regarding who is

speaking about themselves (e.g. this conversation is about them, the next is about you)
- They have an uncanny ability to intuitively know what is going on with you even if you haven't spoken
- They are an HSP or Empath of some sort

The Spiritualist

- Immediate, positive magnetism to them
- They entered your life while you were already on the path of spirituality
- You only speak about things of a spiritual nature (this can include: Astrology, Mysticism, herbalism, the Chakra system, energy, Reiki, the healing arts, tarot, divination, meditation, aromatherapy, sound healing, animal communication, being an Empath, being an HSP, intuition and the clair senses, etc.)
- You may have both come from a very strong Egoic background before you found spirituality
- They are the only one who understands you on your deepest energetic level and never judge you for your beliefs
- They walk with you through Ego Degradation symptoms
- They show you new forms or aspects of spirituality
- They disappear from your life when you are too entangled on the 3D plane
- They live far away

Twin Flames

"THE ORIGIN"

The purpose of Twin Flames

The purpose of Twin Flames is one thing and one thing only. If you've decided to manifest your Twin in this incarnation, it is because you are ready to remember *who and what you are.* You are ready to remember that you are the Universe, you are I AM, you are everything. Meeting your Twin will compound that fact and challenge everything the Ego thought about itself. That includes feelings, beliefs, likes, dislikes, and its false sense of identity.

Your Twin Flame and you are the exact same thing; and when you encounter them, it is an *absolute recognition of yourself as the Universe* (though the mind will fight to ignore it for a while). All of the other Soul Family members play a part in showing your true Self to you, but it is the Twin Flame that bursts the floodgates open and no longer allows the Ego to deny true reality. Because of this, the Twin Flame can be called *The Origin*, for they are you – the originator of all – and the Only.

Just like the belief that Soulmates signify a Soul, Twin Flames are said to be one soul at the beginning of time, which separated and became two. This is incorrect, since again, there is no such thing as a Soul, as everything is One. And just like Soul Tribes, Twin Flames are said to lead the purpose of changing the world together once you've met; that you and your Twin Flame are here to create a "better world" for the rest of humanity on both the 3D and 5D planes. Again, this is completely wrong. To state that the world needs to be "better" is stating that you, the Universe, didn't get it "correct," and now, as a 3D human incarnation, you need another in order to "fix" the problems you created in the first place. It's also insinuating that the world in which we live is the only thing in existence; that there is not a solar system, not a galaxy, not a universe except for the one that you are living in: the microcosm of Ego.

Even though your Twin will enable you to recognize yourself as the Universe, remember that the Ego is a delicate and fragile mirage that can snap under the smallest of breezes, or fight its way tooth and nail to not be annihilated. This duality of how the Ego works and how the Ego perceives is exactly represented within the Twin Flame dynamic between both parties associated. It is what is known as "The Divine Masculine" and "The Divine Feminine," OR, the Runner/Chaser.

It is within the Twin Flame dynamic that we need to really remember that duality is a perception of Ego and does not exist. Twin Flames are spoken about in pure planes of opposite: masculine/feminine; yin/yang; positive/negative; runner/chaser; light/dark. Hopefully this book and the following chapter has or will dispel this concept for you, because when you are dealing with a Twin Flame in particular, it is *imperative* that you recognize the Oneness that you both are. You are the same in every single way, and if you continue to view yourself as separate from your Twin, you will be trapped in the endless cycle of separation/re-union until you both manifest in different incarnations in order to put this incorrect belief to bed.

If you're on a Twin Flame journey, you have manifested an outward personification of yourself – I AM – in order to remember who you are. You have manifested your Twin because you are ready to learn the lessons, do the work, and look at the Ego from an objective standpoint. And if you are on a Twin Flame journey, I know how important this chapter is to you. I know you've been either eagerly reading in order to get to this point, or you've just jumped ahead to get some relief from the pain you're currently in or healing from. I humbly ask, though, that if you skipped ahead to this chapter, it is incredibly important for you to read the rest of the book first: this chapter is a culmination of the rest of the Soul Family, and the first two chapters especially, will help to place this chapter into context. Alternatively, if you are not on a Twin Flame journey and you're just reading this because it's part of the book or because you are curious, try not to feel any way except that you are gaining knowledge. All of us who are on the Twin Flame journey are YOU, and therefore you are experiencing Twin Flames via different Egos which will ultimately transmute into pure I AM energy. You are simply experiencing the Twin Flame journey via the backroads instead of the main highway. And at some point, in this incarnation or 1,000 from now, or anywhere in between or after or before in this non-linear faux timeline you've created, and however you decide to manifest yourself, you will wind up on the main road again. You currently have the beautiful luxury of a scenic drive.

Divine Masculine and Divine Feminine aren't real

Throughout the history of spirituality, there has been the concept of "Divine Masculine" and "Divine Feminine." We see it in Egyptian history with the worship of female deities such as Isis, Hathor, Bastet, Ma'at, and many more, which were then passed down to the more contemporary religions, seen in the Virgin Mary, Aphrodite, Tara, Shakti, etc. These female energies were meant to balance out their masculine counterparts in order to show symmetry within every force. Though they are not technically gender related, the attributes of Divine Feminine have been that of intuition, compassion, nurture, creativity, and sensuality, whereas Divine Masculine qualities have been linked to aggression, money, strategy, and domination. It is noted that when speaking about the Divine Masculine, "He" is always the one that needs to awaken, and the Divine Feminine is always the one who needs to "connect" with Her innate abilities.

The problem with the concepts of Divine Masculine and Divine Feminine is that of Ego. Both rely solely on egoic notions, implying that to end hardness there must be softness, or the antithesis of strategy is creativity. To the egoic mind, these are all true, yet upon Ego Degradation, there is a realization that none of them are accurate, since duality is completely a concept created within the mind. One of the major perceptions (and I repeat that word, *perceptions*) of Twin Flames is that there comes into equity a merging of the Divine Feminine and Divine Masculine; each person representing one of the consorts, and each needing to "awaken" to their own unique divinity via the Ego.

Divine Feminine and Divine Masculine *are not real*, for we are I AM, and there is no duality nor balance when everything is One. The Divine Masculine gaining increased self-esteem, self-confidence, personal power, and sense of purpose through awakening are not solely masculine problems. They are human, egoic constructs that follow the Ego around no matter what faux gender role the internet tells you your spirit is. And the Divine Feminine accessing her heart space, utilizing self-care, and learning to love herself are not solely feminine needs. They are simply egoic throw-away terms of explaining that we need to remember that we are I AM. Because I as the Universe have forgotten myself and am on a journey of remembering through experiencing myself via Ego, I must be told externally ways in which to come back together with I AM that is completely involved through Ego. When we're told "You need to love yourself more," or "You need to practice self-love and self-care," what does that mean? Each Ego distinguishes those terms independently, and when we have nothing to base the concept off of, it ends up becoming a fad term instead of a legitimate method. We also need to remember that each Ego has a Core Karmic lesson, and this is not delineated by opposing energies.

To put it simply, as Twin Flames (and all Soul Family members) are experienced both on the 3D and 5D planes simultaneously, to establish a system of duality between Masculine/Feminine signifies that we are only experiencing the connection on the 3D plane whilst pretending to attend to the 5D. Therefore, as the terms "Divine Masculine" and "Divine Feminine" are incredibly convoluted and full of rhetoric, we will utilize the phrases "Runner" and "Chaser" to symbolize the Twin Flame participants through their 3D actions instead. They are basic, flatlined, and egoic terms that don't pretend to be anything but what they appear.

The terms "Runner" and "Chaser" are utilized on the 3D plane to represent each participant of Twin Flames due to the fact that throughout the journey, one will ultimately run away from the relationship, whereas one will chase the other. Remember that this running and chasing is not happening anywhere except in the 3D realm of Ego, where the concept of separation and attachment are perceived.

These characteristics are generally applied to the "Divine Masculine" as the Runner, and the "Divine Feminine" as the Chaser. The Runner, having more of a proclivity towards Egoic concepts (money, security, foundation, material possessions) are counterintuitive to the Chaser being more interested in emotional notions (intuition, compassion, nurture, spirituality). Regardless of whether you've never "chased" another person before in relationships, nor have ever run from emotions, you may be surprised which one you manifest as once the Twin Flame journey is activated. Along with this, you may also switch positions as going from the Runner to the Chaser, or vice versa, once submission to the journey has occurred.

The Twin Flame "stages"

Each set of Twin Flames are different, as each Ego is different. How you and your Twin manifest your relationship is completely different from how another set of Twins do so. However, though there is not a prescribed set of stages that you will linearly go through in order to reach union, there are a few things that can help you determine whether you are in fact in a Twin Flame relationship. Please keep in mind that these are all signs after interacting with your Twin *in person*, face-to-face. It's an important piece to the energetic calibration that cannot be concrete in a technological relationship.

The Meeting

It is a common misconception that whenever you meet your Twin Flame (TF), you will automatically feel a sense of "home." Not all Twins like the other when they meet, though one is guaranteed to feel the pull immediately. The reason that the feelings may not be mutual initially is because the 5D energy is having a hard time filtering through the 3D plane of Ego, and whatever comes up for that person upon meeting their Twin instinctively puts them off. Meeting a TF is solidifying the energetic link within the 3D plane body, and regardless of what the mind and body feel thus far towards the Twin, the 5D energy has been allied the entire time. Now it's the Ego's responsibility to catch up.

The concept of *mirroring* is introduced in the stage of meeting and may be seen immediately upon such. For example, if you are naturally talkative and open, yet your Twin is generally quiet and reserved, you may find yourselves switching positions during the first in-person interaction. On the flipside, you may be the Twin who feels like you have found your perfect match when you meet your TF for the first time and feel absolutely comfortable, at ease, and at home. The spiritual community calls this an "activation," in which the 5D and 3D planes are properly interacting, and your journey to Awakening is about to begin.

The Muse

Regardless of whether you felt the initial pull from your TF upon physically meeting or not, there is a guarantee that you will feel an absolute spike of creativity almost immediately after. This is the only stage in which you do not have to physically meet your Twin to have the experience. Whether this is via writing poetry, music, creating Fine Art, singing, drawing, dancing, or anything you feel to be creative, both Twins will encounter this musing directly after interacting with their TF. Your energy is trying to release in any way possible, and creativity is the easiest way for it to do so.

The Interjection

Within the first month of meeting your TF face-to-face, there will come a time where I AM energy begins to break through the barrier of Ego, yet the Ego is unaware of it. This is exemplified by the random statements you may make with no thought process behind them. Whether it's blurting out "I love you" and being surprised by your own statement; telling the other person that you're going to marry them someday without knowing why you feel it; or the myriad of other egoically strange things you may say, there will be a time where I AM interjects into the 3D "reality." If you can give justification to why you said or feel what you do, this is not a Twin Flame relationship. The justification does not come until later, after the first separation.

The First Separation

Within two months of meeting your TF in person, you will encounter the first separation. At initial glance, it may seem like any other breakup, argument, fight, or ghosting. But within forty-eight hours, and for both Twins, the feeling that something isn't quite right will hit like a brick wall. Something will feel off. Something will feel *different*. Something will make it feel like you are sinking, and it leads into the next two stages, which will be the crux of your entire Twin Flame journey, until you transcend these stages and come into union.

The Categorization

It is within this first separation that the categories of Runner/ Chaser emerge. It's not solely that the Chaser is the first one to reach out to break separation. It's the *feelings* that create these titles. Within the first separation, both parties concerned will mentally be trying to figure out why they feel the way that they do. Both Twins will be questioning everything they've gone through that's led them up to this point in their lives. Both Twins will want the other back. But the feeling about the process is what delineates between the appellations. Remember that energy does not have duality and it is the Ego and mind that construct it. It is your mind that is filtering feelings, your mind that is generating feelings, and it is only with the initial destruction of the Ego that the next phase occurs, which truly establishes the Chaser for the majority of the journey.

The beginning of true Ego Degradation ("Dark Night of the Soul")

The "Dark Night of the Soul," or 'Oscura Noche' was retroactively given to a poem written in the 16th Century by

Roman Catholic Priest and mystic St. John of the Cross while being imprisoned for his unconventional religious beliefs. In it, he describes the separation of a person's Soul from God. This term is used quite frequently and has become synonymous in the spiritual community with existential crisis, depression, increasing energetic frequency and vibrations, and any type of awakening we encounter whilst learning lessons via the Soul Family. The Dark Night of the Soul is none of these things and is not the correct phrasing to use for the Twin Flame journey at this stage. What is instead happening is the beginning of true Ego Degradation.

Dark Night of the Soul is speaking about a Soul leaving the body and re-uniting with God, as the Other. We have learned that there is no Soul for we are One, and God is "I." Therefore, we can never be separate from "God" because we are the creator, the universe, I AM. There is no ability to separate from the Self except via perception that the Ego creates. And when utilizing the term for Spiritual Awakening, we must remember the context of "Oscura Noche," having been written by a Catholic Priest. The three stages of "Awakening" in Catholicism have to do with salvation through Christ to God's presence. However, salvation in this context cannot occur until physical death, which is made very clear in Biblical texts. If utilizing the term "Dark Night of the Soul" to discuss Karmic lessons being ingrained, we are stating that we cannot be "awakened" until we are physically dead.

Ego Degradation, however, is the ability to witness yourself as the universe, and the deep universal knowledge that you are the same as everything else. It is the deterioration of duality, the understanding that everything is pointless, and the concrete link to the Higher Self that does not enable one to deny or ignore it any longer. And it is within this Ego Degradation during the initial separation between Twins, that the Chaser is born, for they will be the one who experiences it before their TF. It is within this Ego Degradation that the mind begins to freak out and obsess over what it can – 3D perceived tangibility – in order to hold onto control and not be demolished. And it is within this Ego Degradation that the reason for TFs begin to manifest within.

Some of the "symptoms" of Ego Degradation are as such:

- Insomnia or sleeping nonstop*
- Loss of appetite*
- Obsession and rumination*
- Crying out of nowhere, sometimes uncontrollably*
- A feeling of emptiness, hopelessness, helplessness*
- A desire to isolate*
- Irritability and mood swings*
- Nightmares
- Body aches, headaches, digestive upsets*
- A feeling of pressure behind your third eye
- Premonitions, increased sense of smell or hearing, or other heightened clair senses
- The desire to meditate consistently
- The desire to move the body intuitively, such as dance or Yoga
- A feeling like you need to cleanse the inside of the body, or a feeling like you are crawling out of your skin

- Not understanding words anymore when someone speaks to you or when you read something
- Blurry vision, eye pain, or eye ticks
- Loss of memory*
- Dissociation*
- Feeling misunderstood by everyone*
- Feeling absolutely alone and isolated because no one understands you anymore*
- Meeting a Soul Tribe member (especially The Spiritualist)
- Your Soul Family dropping off (especially Soulmates)
- Understanding the *pointlessness* to everything
- Feeling completely lost and not understanding why you've been doing the things that were important to you prior
- Thinking more philosophically
- Unwelcome memories of unhealed trauma
- A loss of faith (if you are religious)
- Beginning to see the falsity in duality
- Realizing that time is not real nor linear
- A severe bout of minimalism (the need to literally purge everything from your life: people, possessions, habits, routines, etc.)
- A drastic switch in diet out of nowhere, like becoming vegan or turning to raw food
- A drastic switch in habits or rituals, like waking up one morning and easily giving up cigarette smoking
- Strong bouts of creativity such as writing, drawing, painting, creating music, etc.
- Becoming more spiritual (not religious)

- Actively looking for a community that can understand the new you
- Researching or reading about philosophical or spiritual topics
- Turning to more esoteric teachings or mysticism

*Any words delineated with a * signify common feelings and symptoms of depression and/or anxiety. Please seek help at your own discretion.*

It is also common within this time frame or directly after, to come across the concept of "Twin Flames." With that being said, it is *only* the Chaser that will come across the sentiment, yet it is very important that they inform the Runner of their findings.

The Re-Union

At this point, after the first separation, the majority of Twins will have a re-union (this is not counting Twins that are married to others, are with others long-term, or who live drastic distances from one another). The re-union between you and your TF is the most cataclysmically divine emotional and energetic feeling you could possibly achieve. The energy is palpable, the Ego is raging, and the emotions are endless. The feeling of absolute bliss is so discernible that it can overwhelm you and take your breath away.

During the first re-union, the dynamic of Runner/Chaser gets even more ingrained, and it is also where the Runner begins to learn their lessons. Runners learn the lessons they need *during union with their Twins*, whereas Chasers learn their lessons *during separation from their Twins*.

This first re-union is also where mirroring becomes ever apparent. You realize that you and your Twin have the same Core Karmic lesson as one another. You recognize that you have the same fears, same deep desires, and that you have been drawn to one another your entire lives, possibly having missed each other in the same location because the Higher Self knew that your 3D Ego was not ready to recognize yourself yet. And as you feel closer and closer to your TF, your Runner TF begins to feel the stirrings of fear. At first subconsciously, and then an absolute panic attack of sorts, where they inevitably run and leave you both in the stage of separation...again. This cycle of separation/re-union may happen over, and over, and over again, or you may stay in separation for years upon years, until you can transcend the Ego.

The Separation

The problem with separation is that it can take over and obsess the mind. Feelings of abandonment, isolation, rejection, aloneness, neglect, and worthlessness can push a person to ruminate and become absolutely consumed, thus believing they have found their TF when in actuality, they have just been triggered by a Karmic. If there is any form of physical abuse, narcissistic abuse, or continuous fighting prior to separation, *this is not your Twin Flame.* Your TF may say some hurtful things based upon their own fears, but there is not a lengthy period of fighting before they turn tail and run.

The true "test" of a Twin Flame comes during the largest stage of separation. Yes, you will most likely feel abandoned, alone, rejected, isolated, neglected, and worthless. But within all of these sentiments begins to blossom something beautiful: self-love. Self-compassion. Self-acceptance. Worthiness. Recognition of I AM. And it's found from self-reflection during the separation period no matter what your Twin is doing. If you begin to feel these things and this internal fire grows, you are so very close to controlling and overcoming the Ego, and you have found your Twin Flame.

The Submission

There will hopefully come a point in which both the Runner and the Chaser reach a stage of submission to the Higher Self. When the Chaser finally stops chasing (both in energy and physicality) and realizes that it doesn't matter whether they are with their TF in the 3D, submission to the journey comes. And when the Runner finally acknowledges that they no longer want to run because there is no escaping themselves, their Ego Degradation begins, and submission to the journey comes. It is *only through submission* that Twins can reach what is called "union."

Union

All of these stages will be spoken about in great detail later in this chapter (including union), but for a brief synopsis, union between Twins is considered to be the end to separation. It is where the Twins "merge" so-to-speak on both the 5D and 3D planes and live out their lives 'Happily Ever After' with one another.

In actuality, union with the Twin is simply union with the Self and a full recognition of I AM energy, since everything – including your Twin – is One. Though it is of course possible and plausible for you to be 'permanently' with your Twin Flame in this incarnation on the 3D plane, the point of manifesting your TF in the first place was not so you could give into Ego and have a romantic relationship. The point was so that you could overcome Ego, no matter how many emotions are present, and remember who I AM.

If you have found your Twin Flame, let there be no doubt that you will 100% meet them face-to-face in this manifestation. There are those out there who have been in contact with another for years via technology only, who believe with all of their hearts that it is their TF they have found, but unless you've met them in person, this is not a Twin Flame. It may be a False Flame, a Karmic, a Soul Mate, or a Soul Tribe Member.

I'm sure this sentiment infuriates some or puts a damper on certain beliefs, but TFs will be pushed towards one another on both the higher and physical planes by the universe, because you have literally manifested them in order to meet. This is why Twins will find one another across oceans, states, and cities; from the middle of nowhere to the most congested of places; from unlikely upbringings to randomly meeting on vacation. TFs will meet in person because it is needed in order to activate the first separation and Ego Degradation through it.

I've heard about people having dreams about their TF and only connecting with them in the 5D for the duration of their lives. This is not a Twin Flame, but the clair senses. I've heard about people talking with their TF across the world for twenty years but never having come into contact with one another in person. This is not a Twin Flame, but a Soulmate. I've heard about people meeting their TF for twenty minutes and never seeing the person again. This is not a Twin Flame, but rather a Karmic. I've heard about people seeing celebrities and fully believing with every fiber of their Being that this person is their TF. It is not a Twin Flame, but an egoic obsession and trauma response. *You must meet and interact with your Twin Flame in person, for an extended period of time, for it to be a Twin Flame.* Otherwise, it's just Ego believing what it wants.

The universe (e.g., "I") will push you and your Twin together in this manifestation. If you have manifested your Twin as married when you meet, this is because you have lessons somewhere in that to learn, and so does your Twin (for example, the married Twin needs to transcend societal constructs that they base their Ego off of, and the other may need to stop looking at 3D relationships for a sense of self-worth). If you and your Twin do the work needed for Ego Degradation, the circumstances will change, and the universe will continue to push you two further together until union can occur...because remember, you ARE the Universe, so you are creating all of this.

The Ego and the Chaser

Within the Twin Flame dynamic, the Chaser does one thing very well...chase. Metaphorically, physically, energetically, and egoically, the Chaser seeks to regain their Twin Flame connection on the 3D plane, and becomes obsessed with the possibility of doing so. What the Chaser doesn't recognize within this, is the desire for control that they are clinging onto, and instead chalk it up to the idea of patience, in which they believe they are going about their own business while patiently waiting for their TF Runner to "realize" that they are in as much pain egoically as the Chaser. However, within this push-and-pull dynamic of energetic exchange, union can never happen with the Twins, for the entire point of the interaction is being missed.

The Chaser is the more open Twin in every fashion. They have most likely undergone some form of Ego Degradation in their life, and are on some form of spiritual journey already. They probably have more heightened clair senses and are aware that they have met some form of Soul Family members within this current incarnation (even if they don't know that they're called such). They probably have learned Karmic lessons and are aware of their Core Karmic lesson, even if they haven't been able to touch the surface of healing it. It's not uncommon for the Chaser to be into mysticism or natural healing modalities, having been propelled into the realm from their past Ego Degradation and the realization that the 3D plane is not the best place to live because it's ephemeral.

The Chaser tends to be more open in their upper chakra system; especially the heart, third eye, and crown chakras. The Chaser may be more flighty; co-dependent; fantastical; idealistic; romantic; vulnerable; communicative; meditative; eccentric; hopeful; trusting; and openly loving than their Twin counterpart. They are highly intuitive, possibly having searched for "something" they couldn't quite put their finger on their entire life. They have possibly been through heartbreak, yet it didn't keep them down for long, for it was more about triggers and trauma responses than true love, and they recognize this with every new Soul Family member they meet. They have a hard time setting boundaries and saying "no," especially when they believe it will hurt another to do so. They have a propensity to always give rather than take, and can get easily drained from allowing their energy to siphon off into various other people, places, and things without proper self-care and energetic protection. They may like themselves outwardly, but have never felt true and unconditional self-love, no matter how much they say they have. The Chaser lives partly in the 5D realm, which is why it's easier for them to access it after they've met the Twin, and they are based primarily in the ethereal realm of dreams, instinct, and emotions rather than just the cold, hard 3D plane.

Meeting the Twin

Remember that at the point of meeting, the delineations between Runner/Chaser have not yet been solidified. However, it is a common misconception that when Twins meet, they will feel immediately at home together. In reality, it's actually very probable that if you don't feel at ease when meeting your Twin, that you will become the Chaser. Just as with the rest of the Soul Family, there is an undeniable magnetism between TFs, but it's not necessarily all positive at first. After all, when the Higher Self recognizes itself as the universe in another 3D manifestation, the Ego does not want to acknowledge it for fear of being destroyed. Therefore, the Ego tries to shut down all recognition and talk you out of being around this person. Alongside this, with the Chaser being so open in their upper chakras, the heart, third eye, and crown chakras begin to protect their energies from the impending "doom" that they perceive is coming...for a Twin Flame relationship is heartbreaking and chalk-full of third party Karmic situations and separations that affect the energy centers negatively until learned to be controlled.

Though the Ego may be screaming that you are not interested, there could feel to be a type of cord that keeps you curious about the Twin. It's not felt yet anywhere near as strongly as it will be felt in the future upon separation, but the feeling of *je ne sais quoi* still nags at the corner of your Being. If the Twins touch upon first meeting, the sensations will be explosive. For the Chaser, it will not be the same as when touching a Karmic or Soulmate, for those impressions are electric and thrilling. For the Chaser touching their Twin for the first time, it may possibly be terrifying, confusing, shocking, and hesitant. The Ego at this point is fighting tooth and nail to not get attached, and to try to understand what is happening since the sensations and the thoughts are not linking up. The only way for the Chaser to perceive what is happening at this stage is through the Ego, and the Ego itself is aghast at the possibility of being subdued, which will ultimately happen when recognizing I AM energy.

With the first meeting comes the first sign of mirroring. Though you may not understand what is happening consciously at first, a large part of Egoic dislike or confusion with the Twin stems from them acting *just like you*. This is happening to show the Higher Self how you are perceived through the lens of others. For example, you may be an incredibly open person, sharing your life history at the drop of a hat, but upon meeting your Twin, you may present yourself as secretive, whereas the TF expresses secrets they've never told anyone before. This mirroring gives a glimpse into what the Twin feels and senses, how they will normally act, and their perception of your Egoic self. The Ego can then inspect things on the first-glance synthesis of your mask towards the world, and notice things that may be desired to be changed. When mirroring occurs at first meeting, it is the most topical and benign form of mirroring you will have with the TF. It is a tiny taste of what is to come.

After the first meeting for the Chaser, is what I like to call *The Muse* phase. For the Chaser specifically, once they meet their TF face-to-face, their sacral and crown chakras metaphorically explode, and creativity begins to burst out of them. However one deems creativity or any creative proclivities is how this will manifest: writing, painting, drawing, singing, sculpting, building, etc. Whether you liked your Twin or not upon meeting has no bearing on this element...if you find yourself in the throes of creative passion upon meeting, you have met your TF. This "stage" is part of the beautiful ability for the Chaser to begin self-love and recognizing themself as I AM. The creative energy is so strong and so seemingly out of nowhere, that it begins to settle into the Chaser's consciousness that even though their Ego may not have liked the TF the first time around, something *is* in fact different about them. Note that just because something feels different does not mean it is a TF; the rest of the Soul Family will feel different as well; it is important to recognize *all* signs for a TF, not just pick and choose between them.

At this point, it's common for the Twin who felt comfortable during the first meeting to actively chase the other. It allows the Twins to link their energies more deeply on the 5D plane, and also enables the 3D plane to acknowledge what is happening at the level of the Higher Self. Within the first few weeks upon meeting face-to-face, there will be a seemingly random proclamation of grandiosity such as a declaration of love; a statement that there will be a marriage in the future between the Twins; or something absolutely jarring when heard out loud. This is different than a Soulmate where the energy feels complete, and it's different than a Karmic where the random declaration of love may feel 'right' and 'good.' This is an energy that doesn't make sense to either party when it's stated, yet for some reason, it's still being shared vocally. Either or both Twins may partake in these bombastic verbalizations, and either or both Twins will undoubtedly be shocked at their own announcement. In this "stage," the Higher Self is beginning to poke holes through the Ego, and it's occurring so quickly, that the Ego cannot keep up with what's happening. An averment of love, for example, may not be so positive to the broadcaster, but rather confusing, bewildering, and put them on edge. In fact, they may not even physically feel this love yet, but they've stated it out of the blue and it's only a matter of time before the body syncs up with the 5D. It is the first time both Twins will notice (albeit maybe not consciously acknowledge it) the fragility of the Ego and the false perceptions it encapsulates.

Separation for the Chaser

Upon the first separation, the delineations of "Runner" and "Chaser" come to fruition. This first separation happens within two months of meeting one another face-to-face, and it must happen in order to get the Twins on the path of recognizing I AM, feel self-love as the universe manifested in physical form, and truly begin Ego Degradation. Even though the Twins may not speak on the 3D plane during this time, both parties begin to feel the invisible link that has connected them, and they both begin to feel as if something is "wrong." The first one who reaches out to the other has now been categorized as "The Chaser" in energetic terms, and it's not because they solely physically chased, but because they were the first to realize and express their unhappiness in not being around the other. They've begun to awaken. Please understand this sentence to its fullest: *the Chaser heals during separation.*

During separation, the Chaser will be the first to begin their Ego Degradation. As stated previously, this can appear to have the same symptoms as depression, so it's imperative to make sure that what is being felt is not in fact depression, first and foremost. It's very common to feel depression symptoms with members of the Soul Family, especially Karmic relationships and Soulmates. It's also common to feel them at the beginning of a Twin Flame journey, notably for those who have a predisposition towards such mental ailments. But the more that the Ego degrades, the more any form of depression symptoms begin to fade, even if one has had depression their entire lives.

Ego Degradation for the Chaser will occur quicker and more intensely if they have already undergone some form of Ego Degradation prior in this incarnation. At the beginning, the Ego does not understand what is going on with the 5D energy that is being felt with the TF, as it is not used to being synced with 3D plane "realism," thus it attempts to grasp at anything it can. This is where the obsession and rumination for the physical person of the Runner Twin occurs. The 5D energy that is experienced so strongly, gets trapped on the 4D bridge of filter, and all that is left is a deep knowing that the relationship between Twins is not over. The awareness that the relationship is not over is always true, for TFs can never be separated in energy, but the Ego has a tendency to cling onto it, not interpreting the difference between planes, and fully deny the 3D "reality" of the situation. This is where the danger lies for the Chaser, for inability to accept the situation as it is, is what keeps the Chaser in chaser mode for an indefinite amount of time.

Obsession with the Runner Twin is the worst part egoically of being on a Twin Flame journey. The pull is so devastatingly strong, that the Chaser may find themselves not able to function or think about anything else besides being with the Twin. This is obsession found on the deepest level, at the core of the energetic Being, to the point that the Chaser will do anything and everything they can to "forget" about the Runner. This is also where the notion of "cutting the cord" comes into play, for the Chaser will energetically feel and know that there is an invisible thread tethering the two together, and attempt to "cut" this cord. However, the Twins are *the same thing*, so one cannot cut a cord with the Self. You have manifested your Twin to show you who you are, to remember I AM, and what is simply being felt is the interconnectedness to all, that "I" has created. The beautiful part of the obsessive characteristics within the Twin Flame journey is what undeniably happens on the unseen level: the link between 5D and 3D energy, whereby the Ego obsesses over the Twin due to the energy, and the two inevitably link up, creating a form of healing for the Chaser.

If there is any contact between the Twins during the time of obsession, the Chaser will undoubtedly have hundreds of questions. The Chaser, during separation, has been trying to grapple with their Ego and its protection of itself so it does not get decimated. As the Ego likes to create linearity; patterns; dualities; reasons; understandings; and logical, concrete conclusions, it will hold onto any and all inference as to why the TF is running, and why the Chaser can bring them back. The questions posed to the Runner, however, energetically exhaust them, for it is pulling 5D energy down into the 3D, and thereby grounding the Runner more in their lower chakras of Ego. It's completely understandable why the Chaser has so many questions, as the Ego attempts to "know" what is going on, but let this be a reminder that what the Runner is saying regarding their running, is not necessarily the actuality of the matter. Aside from a bombardment of questions, the Chaser may also believe that if they tell their Twin their newfound "realizations" about themselves, the Twin, or their journey together, that the Runner will change their ways and remain with the Chaser. But as the Runner has not even begun their Ego Degradation as of yet, these conclusions will simply fall on deaf ears, and the Chaser remains in chaser energy. However, it is important that once you have clarified to yourself that you are on a TF journey, that you let the Runner know so it may begin sinking in. It may not be received well, but in time, it will be understood once the Runner begins to heal their own traumas.

For the Chaser during separation, they begin to feel the Runner energetically so strongly, that it becomes overpowering. It's very common to have connection 'signs' that show the Chaser that they are still tethered to the Runner in the 5D that manifest in the 3D. These are the nine most common signs:

<u>Feeling them empathically</u>: The Chaser may be going about their business, having put a task to the forefront of their mind instead of obsession over the Runner, and all of a sudden a gut-punch of emotion comes up. This could be anger, sadness, confusion, or longing, and the feeling does not belong to them. The recognition that they are empathically feeling the Twin is prevalent, and it is happening because they, for a brief moment, were not in chaser energy.

<u>Dreams in the 5D</u>: These are not dreams in which the Chaser goes through hypothetical, dream-like scenarios with the Runner, or dreams about something traumatic or lovely from the past or a projection into the future. These are dreams in which the Chaser wakes up feeling like they have just spent the entire night with the TF. There is a sense of deep peace upon waking, for the Twins have just participated in connection on the 5D plane for the duration or part of the night.

<u>The Soul Family activates the connection more</u>: Spending any amount of time with any other member of the Soul Family is absolutely exhausting. The Chaser has surpassed the lessons that the previous Soul Family members were meant to teach them, and being around their energy is like being sucked into a vortex of Egoic hell.

<u>Small talk is exhausting</u>: Just the prospect of having small talk with anyone is too much to bear. The absolute exhaustion of talking about 3D concepts, ideas, or Egoic jargon makes the Chaser want to crawl into a hole. This is part of Ego Degradation, and it's also completely opposite to how the Runner is functioning. If you are feeling this symptom, the Runner is most likely engaging in third-party situations at this point.

<u>Feeling and seeing their 'color:'</u> Unconsciously, the Chaser has probably designated a color to their Runner Twin. When thinking about your Twin, what color comes to mind? Is it light blue? Emerald green? Magenta? Sunshine yellow? When the color is defined, sit and do a full-body scan of yourself. Go inch-by-inch concentrating on your body, your form, what you see in your mind, the feeling of your feet on the floor. Next, do a full-body scan again, and sense if you can feel or see the color of your Twin attached to your body somewhere. This is the most surefire way to recognize that you are connected to one another and that their energy is with you. Their energy has literally attached to yours, and within that energy, you are experiencing their stuff along with yours.

At this point, it's time to get rid of their energy, because as you focus on yourself and your own growth, you do not need to be sifting through your Twin's stuff as well. Concentrate on their color on your body, and using a metaphorical and large mind-squeegee, push all of that colored energy down through your body and out through the soles of your feet, seeing the energy go back to your TF. Keep doing this until all of their color is gone from your energy field. Then, with your feet on the floor, pull up through the soles of your feet pure, white light energy. This practice is taught to energy healers to help cleanse and clear their energetic fields, and it will make you feel emotionally and energetically better once you remove all energy but your own from your system.

<u>Flashes of what they're doing</u>: Especially when the Chaser has begun to detach their obsessive thinking from the physical person of the Runner, this 'sign' is one of the stranger ones. The Chaser may be doing something of their own accord when all of a sudden they visually see what is around the Runner and what the Runner is visually seeing through their own eyes. It generally only lasts a few seconds, but it is as if the Chaser is in the Twin's body.

<u>Heightened energy overload</u>: If the Runner comes physically closer to the Chaser in any form, the feeling of their energy around is heightened and can be overwhelming. The Chaser may know when the Runner is in their neighborhood, nearby, or if they don't live in the same state, if they travel to a closer proximity.

<u>Know when they're trying to pull away</u>: The same as above, but on the flipside, when the Runner tries to detach their energy from the Chaser, the Chaser feels it as if a cord is pulling their heart out of their chest and they're being dragged along with it. Remember that the 'cord' can never be broken since I AM is One, but when there is an intention by either Twin to detach their energy in any fashion, the other will feel it. This goes both ways, and yes, the Runner feels it when the Chaser attempts it as well. This is also felt if the Runner moves physically further

away from the Chaser (say, going on vacation). The Chaser may feel the Runner's energy pull away when they leave, and then have a heightened energy overload when they return.

<u>Synchronicities</u>: If you follow my teachings, you'll know I do not like to talk about synchronicities very much, since the Ego can perceive them however they want and give them false meanings. But there are certain times in separation when synchronicities and signs can no longer be ignored regarding the TF, and they usually occur in repetition and sequentially. This can be things such as: hearing alarms going off; seeing repeating numbers (especially 1's, 2's, and 4's); having a wild animal show up over and over next to you or in your immediate vicinity (like hummingbirds, mourning doves, crows; or butterflies); seeing the Twin's name on random things repetitively; and listening to the radio and the sequence of music tells the story of your relationship. Be careful with your interpretation of synchronicities, because it generally is the Ego seeing what it wants to see. However, it can also pertain to the Higher Self and Ego linking up like a clair sense.

What the Chaser needs to overcome

With the Chaser being so open in their upper chakras, there are general problems that they have on the 3D plane with setting boundaries and too much selflessness to the point of detriment. Though both Twins will have the same Core Karmic lesson that they each need to learn in their own way, usually the apparent issues that the Chaser needs to overcome are as follows: co-dependency; abandonment; feeling like they are not priority; lack of self-love; lack of self-worth; over-sharing; lack of boundaries; not being grounded; selflessness; expectations; and not trusting in Divine Timing.

The entirety of this list consists of Egoic problems that may be fixed outwardly through the help of the other Soul Family members or on one's own, however, they are deeply ingrained patterns of childhood trauma or trauma repetition that instill to the core these fears and beliefs. Meeting the TF will help to extinguish the fears and trauma responses, however, the Chaser will notice that the items on this list will be ever-present during the times of separation and chasing. In actuality, these fears are what drive the chasing, and there is no one like a TF to surface the knowledge that the Chaser does in fact have deep traumas that need to be healed in this incarnation.

It may help to give an example to showcase how a TF relationship can affect the Chaser and their Core Karmic lesson:

Andy is the Chaser and his Core Karmic lesson is self-worth. He has just gotten back into re-union with his Twin Flame. Due to having felt abandoned from his Twin running, having triggered a lack of self-worth, Andy begins to showcase co-dependent traits. Within this co-dependency comes a tendency to act selflessly and give too much of himself even though he is still hurting from the sting of separation. Andy over-shares everything he thinks and feels so that his Twin can "know" everything going on and possibly not run anymore. Andy also has zero boundaries with his Twin because he doesn't want to push him into running again. Andy is now very dissociated because he's trying to keep his Twin with him in the 3D while simultaneously undergoing Ego Degradation and attempting to sift through his own 3D trauma. All of this finds Andy feeling like he's not a priority, which ultimately hits his Ego and Andy begins having large expectations of what he wants his Twin Flame journey to look like. Andy's Twin runs again, and Andy is once more left feeling abandoned with a complete lack of self-worth because he did everything he could to be the "perfect partner." Andy scrambles to figure out how and when his TF will return, obsessing over it day and night.

All of these things that Andy felt and did are very common with regards to a TF Chaser. Because meeting a TF – an absolute recognition of yourself as the universe – is meant to cripple the Ego and dismantle all sense of "lack" in this falsely dualistic illusion the mind has created. Andy's triggers and trauma responses are not healed yet. But if he's being triggered when he is in re-union with his TF, then how can he truly heal? The answer is to enter into separation again, which is where the TF Chaser heals. And the Higher Self will make sure that happens, leading Andy to submission and surrender to the journey.

The Ego and the Runner

Within the TF dynamic, the Runner does one thing very well: avoid...for as long as they can, as much as they can, and for as long as they can justify it. What the Runner doesn't realize about this, however, is that they are trying to outrun themselves, their past traumas, triggers, and their 3D perceived reality of what makes them comfortable instead of the necessary growth they need to overcome their demons. The Runner will justify to themselves why they cannot move forward, but instead remain in the same place they have been – sometimes for decades – in order to not get hurt or triggered again. When they meet their TF, they are so emotionally and energetically overwhelmed that they push them away in hopes of regaining some control over their own emotions and proving to themselves and everyone else that they do not 'need anyone;' feeling such a lack of self-love and self-worth that they are convinced they, themselves, are the only ones reliable.

The Runner is more closed off than the Chaser. It is not uncommon for the Runner to know absolutely nothing about energy, and not believe in it whatsoever. They have a more analytical and scientific mind, needing proof regarding anything spiritual. Though their clair senses may have guided them through a large portion of their life, the Runner is blind to it, and chalk it up to either good instincts, intelligence, learned information, or pattern recognition. Instead of learning Karmic lessons in a mellow manner, the Runner may have a tendency to take their responses to extremes: stonewalling instead of communicating; closing off instead of listening; running instead of trying to understand. The Runner has definitely encountered many Soul Family members in their life (though not as much as the Chaser), but they are oblivious to the purpose of them and therefore prefer to shut down their emotions when a lesson is being shown. The Runner lives completely on the 3D plane of their perceived reality, and have thwarted themselves towards anything mystical, esoteric, or spiritual. They may also have a severe distaste for religion, community, and tradition; anything that requires trust in something other than their own Ego.

The Runner tends to be more open in their lower chakra system; especially the root, sacral, and solar plexus chakras. The Runner may be more grounded; independent; 'realistic;' analytic; stern; brooding; invalidating; quiet; closed-off; scientifically minded; complacent; stubborn; responsible; obliged; un-trusting; and self-loathing than their Twin counterpart. They are highly emotional yet keep it hidden from the world, and have probably been secretly searching for "something" their entire lives that they attributed to money, work, or prestige. They have most likely been through heartbreak by a Karmic that crushed their hope for the future and made them retreat more into their shell, for they did not learn their lesson, but rather turned the situation back onto themselves and transmuted it into self-loathing. They are trigger-happy with setting boundaries, sometimes setting them too staunchly, yet having no problem crossing others'. They have a propensity to neither give nor take, for they believe that their microcosm of Ego is all they need, so they isolate their emotions and don't develop deeply meaningful relationships with others as they age. They play it safe always, and possibly have a hard time making decisions unless they've thought about them for an exponentially long period of time. They may act like they love themselves outwardly (sometimes appearing narcissistic), but have a deep sense of self-loathing and lack of self-worth that they do not show until they meet their TF. The Runner lives completely in the 3D realm until they encounter their Twin, which propels them quickly into the realm of 5D which they fight and run from until they no longer can.

Meeting the Twin

When the Runner is asked how they felt upon first meeting their TF in physicality, they'll most likely say "I felt like I was home." Interestingly enough, the premise that TFs always feel comfortable upon meeting is generally geared towards what the Runner felt, and this gets confused later on with how the Chaser feels in separation. This very reason is why TFs need to meet in person in order to "activate" the TF dynamic: the Runner needs to feel the energy and be encompassed by the physicality of their Twin in order for their healing work to begin, as they are more open in the lower chakras, also known as the chakras of Ego. Unfortunately, this overtake of energy is also what makes the Runner run, since the emotions are too powerful to experience solely on the 3D plane, which is where the Runner resides. This is why the Runner is mostly *physically* attracted to their Twin upon meeting. This physical attraction is actually an energetic attraction, but the Runner does not understand this yet.

Upon first meeting and even prior, the undesignated Runner will in fact more than likely be the one who is chasing their TF for a relationship. It can therefore be said that whomever shows the most interest at the beginning of the journey will become the Runner. This is important for two reasons: firstly, the Runner Twin needs to *want* a relationship or connection with their Twin in order for them to stick around through the cycles of the TF journey; and secondly, this chasing from the Runner both begins the TF cycles of separation and re-union, and ends them finishing with union if they are able to reach that point. The Runner is the one who starts and finishes the 3D sojourn, whereas the Chaser connects them to the 5D.

Prior to the first meeting for the Runner, is again, *The Muse* phase. As the Chaser doesn't really acknowledge this energy and explosion of the sacral chakra until they physically meet their Twin, the Runner can experience it prior to meeting their Twin. As the Runner is more open in the lower chakras, their creative energy is more able to flow when they are hit with any emotion, and just speaking to their TF will begin to open the floodgates of their heart and third eye chakras in order for this creative energy to burst forth. Chances are they will not outwardly state how their TF has inspired ingenuity in them unless asked, but as they tend to be more creatively closeted, they are more used to emotions guiding their sacral chakra. If the Runner did not speak to their TF prior to meeting them, their clair senses possibly guided them to begin unlocking their imaginativeness without any knowledge of why. *The Muse* stage is part of the Runner's journey to begin letting emotions and energy flow through them instead of bottling them up and pushing them down. Meeting their TF, the Runner's sacral chakra begins to come into balance, and their over-zealous sexuality, sexual energy, and creativity start to smooth out. Just as it is a constant fight for the Chaser to bring their heart chakra into balance upon meeting their TF, it is the same for the Runner and their sacral chakra. As the sacral chakra is characterized traditionally by the lotus flower representing the cycles of birth, death, and rebirth, the Runner is here shown again to begin the TF journey on the 3D plane.

At this point, the Runner has begun chasing their TF, since they felt an absolute recognition of Self and a complete comfortability upon meeting. Within the first few weeks upon meeting face-to-face, there will, again, be a seemingly random proclamation of grandiosity. It is here where the Runner begins to feel two things: the first are deep feelings of love for the TF, which conclusively becomes self-love, as they are beginning to connect with the Higher Self which is initiating its breakdown of the Ego. The second is fear, caution, skepticism, and unsureness as the Ego grips for dear life to not be subdued or broken. Though these feelings may not be completely conscious yet, the Ego plants a seed of doubt within the Runner's mind, and since the Runner has no conscious experience with the Higher Self, they allow the Ego to take over. It is within the next month that the first separation will undoubtedly occur.

Separation for the Runner

The first separation occurs and the Twins are about to be delineated with their 3D titles. At this point, the Runner will do everything to rationalize how they can easily live without the Chaser, and "why" it is so much better to be without them. Though the Runner senses deep feelings within their Being for the Chaser, their Ego is still the predominant driving force to their lives, and the seed of fear that was planted during the proclamation of love begins to grow into a sapling. In the first separation, the Runner will justify to themselves why the relationship with their TF will not work, and mentally construct an infinite amount of reasons as to why it's better that the relationship ended before it became too intense. If the Ego and the 3D situations are too glaring, it is possible that there will not be a reunion at the point of the Chaser reaching out. If the 3D constructs don't have an additional hindrance (such as marriage or distance), the Twins will most likely enter into reunion once the Chaser reaches out. How the Runner reacts in separation will be the same regardless.

When in separation, the Runner never reaches out to the Chaser. They know that the Chaser has a bevy of questions, but they're unable to answer them. The reason for this, is because I AM energy has manifested the Twin and the separation in order to grow and expand. The questions the Chaser has regarding the separation are the Ego attempting to grapple with the 3D situation at hand, but since the Twins are now heavily linked on the 5D as well as the 3D, the Egoic questions in actuality don't have answers to them. The Runner keeps their distance on the 3D plane due to their own fears, trauma, and the belief that they are doing the Chaser a favor by staying away; and on the 5D plane because they are themselves growing and expanding, since they are the same thing as the Chaser, who is growing and expanding during separation.

If discussed solely through the Ego, it is one of the most frustrating things to not ever hear from the Runner. If TFs enter into separation over and over again, the Chaser will hold onto the hope that the Runner will reach out to them, no matter how many times they've participated in the same cycle. This is in part due to the fact that the Runner chased them at the beginning of the relationship, so it is confusing to the Ego. However, this leads only to a bombardment of overwhelm and accumulated emotional pain that usually has the Chaser continuously "break down" and reach out. To understand why the Runner does not reciprocate in chasing, it's important to view it through the lens of the Core Karmic lesson, for this is what is being worked on through these separations and reunions, both in the Runner and the Chaser, since the Core Karmic lesson is identical in both.

When you've truly manifested a TF, the Core Karmic lesson in this incarnation will be either self-love or self-worth. There may be a pepper of abandonment issues, boundaries, or mindfulness symptoms as well. In this case, it's easier to see how the Runner, upon feeling the strength of emotions emanating from the Chaser, will view the situation as a "threat" to themselves, since their lack of self-love and self-worth become amplified upon meeting the TF. This is a main reason that Runners run: because they feel that they will lose control of their lives and their emotions if they interact with the Chaser, and feel that separation is necessary in order to live and regain that "normal" life they had prior to meeting. The Runner feels like their emotions have been exposed in some way, and this leads to perpetual running in order to regain that sense of false control they believed they had over their own lives preceding TF synergy.

When in separation and desperate to communicate, the Runner will still hold off, believing that they would be disturbing the Chaser and their life. They also deeply believe that they do not "deserve" the Chaser, as they continuously feel less than and insecure in comparison due to the way the Chaser is able to open the floodgates of Runner emotions. The Runner is aware of their patterns, how they feel and what they want, but at this point, are not able to release their Egoic control over themselves. The Runner truly just wants the Chaser to be happy, and they believe themselves to be so "damaged," that they are not able to be the one to make the Chaser happy. TFs are heavily linked even in separation, and until both completely let go in all aspects, the Runner cannot have their Ego Degradation.

What the Runner needs to overcome

With the Runner being so grounded in their lower chakras, there are general problems that they have on the 3D plane with attachment to material and Egoic proclivities to the point of detriment. Though both Twins will have the same Core Karmic lesson that they each need to learn in their own way, usually the apparent issues that the Runner needs to overcome are as follows: aloofness; selfishness; abandonment; lack of self-love; lack of self-worth; lack of communication; fear of weakness, or pride; vices (Karmic situations); rigidity; control; and complacency, or the feeling of obligation, which leads them to not fight for what they want.

The entirety of this list consist of Egoic problems that may be fixed outwardly through the help of the other Soul Family members or on one's own, however, they are deeply ingrained patterns of childhood trauma or trauma repetition that instill to the core these fears and beliefs. Meeting the TF will in fact help to extinguish the fears and trauma responses, however, the Runner will notice that the items on this list will be ever-present during the times of re-union and whilst running. As stated previously, these fears are what drive the running, and it is the meeting and interaction with the TF which surface the recognition that the Runner's sublimation of their own traumas has done nothing but kept them in a perpetual state of isolation.

On the contrary to "Andy's" synopsis above, let's look at an example of his Twin Runner to showcase how a TF relationship can affect the Runner and their Core Karmic lesson:

> *Patrick is the Runner and his Core Karmic lesson is self-worth. He has just gotten back into reunion with Andy, after Andy reached out to him. Though Patrick is egoically happy and at peace currently, Andy seems to be more clingy, needy, and hesitant around Patrick. Andy is also consistently trying to express to Patrick*

how important their relationship is and what it "should" look like, and Patrick feels an undue amount of pressure and stress from it because he doesn't believe he can live up to what Andy wants. Andy's constant praising of Patrick and proclamation of undying love for him makes Patrick feel like Andy is putting him on a pedestal; one he can never attain. Though Andy doesn't express them out loud, Patrick feels that Andy has put a lot of expectations on both the relationship and Patrick in general, and he begins to become afraid that he will let Andy down. All of this leaves Patrick feeling like it's just a matter of time before Andy realizes that Patrick isn't worth the salt he's selling, and will ultimately hurt Patrick. To Patrick, it's better to take care of his own life and allow Andy to find someone who will be worthy of the relationship. Patrick runs, with the justification in his head that Andy expected too much and wanted too much. Now Patrick does what he can to occupy and distract himself, hoping that in time, these deep feelings for Andy will subside.

All of these things that Patrick felt and did are very common with regards to the Runner, since TF relationships are meant to mirror to each party the Core Karmic lesson needing to be healed, and showcase the triggers, which are doorways into that healing. As Runners heal during re-union, Patrick's triggers appear strongly when he and Andy are together. When they are apart, he attempts to distract himself and justify to himself why the relationship will not work. It is not until chaser energy subsides on Andy's side that Patrick can begin to degrade the Ego and truly work on his Core Karmic lesson, finally submitting to the journey.

The importance of separation

Though separation is the hardest part of the TF journey, it is also the most imperative part next to actually meeting the Twin. The lessons that the Runner learned energetically and subconsciously within reunion with the Chaser are now being ingrained into their lives, and the Chaser has the room to heal their own Core Karmic lesson and work on healing themselves. In order to do this, a few things occur, and this is why TFs enter into separation over and over again.

First, we must remember that there is actually no such thing as true separation because TFs are the *exact same thing* – I AM. Therefore, separation really only occurs within the frame of the Ego and its perception of pain and distance based upon what it believes it can see. Separation, in this case, is really just a *feeling* of being apart, for in actuality, you can never separate from yourself. The distinction between "I" and Ego, however, is very prevalent, and it is within and from TF separation that these two worlds can finally fully bridge and merge together into "union." For this union to occur, TFs must first recognize and realize that separation from the 3D physical manifestation of the Twin is happening for a reason. It's not a punishment, it's not the universe turning its back, and it's not Karma. It's the Higher Self granting the gift of Awakening, for a separation from a TF is one of the fastest and best ways to remember who I AM and cultivate the healing work to ameliorate the Core Karmic lesson. These things will happen on their own after meeting the TF, but it is each party's responsibility to mindfully balance and sublimate the Ego in the process.

Why the Runner runs

Let's be honest. If the Runner didn't run, there would be no separation between TFs, however, without them running, there would be no Ego Degradation on either side, nor would TFs be as universally powerful as they are. The Runner may run in physicality, emotionality, mentally, and even attempt to run energetically. The problem the Runner faces within the relationship with their TF is that they do not want to be in pain from connecting so deeply with the Chaser. The Runner functions on the level of the mind, and the pure recognition of I AM and facing the mirror being held up to them by the Chaser is too much for their Ego to bear. The Ego then makes the Runner "see" why they should leave the relationship, but in reality, the Runner doesn't understand yet that the Twins met in order to trigger healing in one another. So they listen to the Ego and justify their running utilizing surface reasoning.

When TFs are together, the Runner feels "exposed" due to their feelings towards the Chaser, trying to understand it with the only tool they have in their arsenal: logic. Because of this, the Runner always feels like they are "less than" the Chaser: less than in ability to express feelings, less than in spiritual growth, less than in communication, less than in any and all ways. As the Runner is more open in the lower chakras, they begin to try to "better themselves" on the physical plane in order to "prove their worth" to the Chaser, which is ultimately, themself. This is why the Runner is attached to Egoic notions of money, prestige, pride, power, control, intelligence, and legacy. But even when these things are obtained, the Runner still does not feel worthy enough of their TF, and so they run. Directly after running, the Runner will immediately feel relieved, safer, and as if life is and will be easier. This will all shift once Ego Degradation begins to occur, and self-love and self-worth blossom in the Runner.

TFs are exact mirrors of one another as they are an absolute recognition of yourself as I AM. To understand how you fit into the 3D plane, the TF shows you who you are perceived to be by mirroring you in most forms. This could be mirroring a past or current version of you. Since TFs have the same Core Karmic lesson, each party will live through the same tests and need to eliminate the same aspects of their egoic selves, although, these tests come at different points for each Twin Ego, since time is not linear. Each test presented is meant to show on the 3D plane that TFs are synonymous, and on the 5D plane to heighten awareness and remove boundaries of Ego. TFs also reflect Egoic habits that need to be ended, using projection as the main authority. For example, if the Runner calls the other controlling whilst themselves having immense control issues. Or if the Runner is perpetually fearful of getting cheated on whilst themselves cheating on the Chaser. *Whenever a Twin points a finger, they're pointing it at themselves.* All of the things that either Twin dislikes about themselves and attempts to run from or ignore, are the very issues that need to be healed either via Ego Degradation, Third Party Situations, or mindfulness practice.

Dating others/Third Parties

Third Party Situations are anything egoic and external that hinder the remembrance of I AM within a TF journey. Whether this is workaholism; continuous familial or friend distrust of the Twin; preoccupation with 3D distractions; or another person getting in the way, Third Parties are an important part of the journey for the Runner to begin having their Ego Degradation, and for the Chaser to build non-attachment. Third Parties are still a form of running for the Runner and co-dependency for the Chaser, and just as stated in the section on Karmic relationships, if I AM is not expanding and growing, or the Ego is complacent, the Higher Self will send something in to shake things up. This is where Third Party Situations occur, which are really Karmic lessons being recounted. However, just because it's important and common on the 3D plane, it is completely up to each Twin whether they want to continue and persist in the TF relationship for their own energetic, mental, and physical well-being and health. Just because one is on a TF journey does not mean that either party has to be all right with everything that occurs within said journey. That is the beautiful part of the Ego: the ability to choose.

It is still incredibly common for Karmics to enter the lives of TFs after having found one another. Lessons still need to be learned, and as we know, Karmics are the fastest way to learn these lessons. If not a Karmic person, then a Karmic lesson may enter in the form of a Soulmate or group lesson (such as a lesson learned at work or from a group of people). If one or both of the TFs are partnered already, their Karmic lessons from their partner will be more forthcoming. To the Ego, Third Parties are incredibly hurtful for and towards the Twins, but it will also aid in bringing about Ego Degradation for both Egos, since they will provide a hard lesson in universal reality.

Though it is always difficult for the heart to date another when we have our sights set on someone else, there are specific things that occur after you've met the TF and attempt to be with another Soul Family member or non-Soul Family member. These things can occur with anyone in your life and anyone that you meet, including those you are not intimate with, and those that have been in your life for a long period of time (such as Soulmates). Please remember that it is natural for the Ego to compare, as it likes duality, so these feelings can be present if obsessing over a Karmic or Soulmate. However, with a Karmic or Soulmate, these feelings can be pushed through over time, whereas with a TF, these feelings never go away after interaction with the TF. Here are five things that commonly occur when trying to date another after interacting with the Twin:

<u>Constant intuition:</u> Both Twins will encounter things like dreams, visions, and feeling their Twin energetically and/or

physically. This is happening because there is a dissociation between 3D and 5D energy where the Ego is trying to move on, but the 5D energy is still attached.

<u>Not enough attraction:</u> Neither Twin will be able to get attracted enough to others in any and all aspects, nor will they be able to sustain a consistent attraction. The Ego gets attracted, but the energy gets bored. Both Twins will ultimately feel bored with any type of surface relationships.

<u>The energetic bond "issue:"</u> A lot of TFs will try to break the energetic bond they feel with their TF, which is called "cutting the cord." Attempting to cut the cord through meditation, rituals, distractions, etc. will not only reinforce the energetic connection to the TF, but it will physically deplete the body. This also occurs if a TF is in a Third Party Relationship with a Karmic or a Soulmate plus Karmic, as the Karmic lessons are so low in frequency at this point, that it manifests in the body. This can be seen as depression, exhaustion, insomnia, lack of appetite, lack of sex drive, lack of motivation, and desire for isolation. The attempt at energetic bond breaking also blocks intuition, creativity, and clair senses, as it locks up the Sacral chakra. An endeavor to break the bond with the TF is in actuality an experimentation in separating from yourself, as you and your Twin Flame are the same I AM energy.

<u>Misunderstood:</u> Both Twins will feel misunderstood by anyone aside from their TF, and as if no one can understand them ever again. The Soul Family will feel familiar, yet still won't be able to penetrate the emotions deep enough. Both Twins will feel a sense of disinterestedness with anyone aside

from their TF. If a TF attempts to date a Soulmate, the Soulmate will either bore the Twin to tears or enrage them with their form of communication. The Soulmate will be too involved in their own Ego and 3D plane falsities for the Twin to stand being around them (this is a balance of the Root Chakra). Both TFs will feel a sense of longing whilst being with anyone but each other. Though the energy with a Karmic or Soulmate is still in the 5D, the vibrations after meeting the TF are so high that nothing else resonates. Prior to meeting the TF, it's much easier to feel more fulfilled in these other two types of Soul Family relationships because there's no awareness yet of what depth TF relationships have.

<u>The Runner will always be looking for the Chaser:</u> The Runner will always be searching for the Chaser in others, whether these people are Karmics, Soulmates, or Soul Tribe Members. They will compare the Third Party person logically to the TF and most likely be completely cut off energetically from anyone else. Once the Runner realizes no one feels the same as being around the Twin, they will end their Third Party relationship.

TFs are game changers. Once TFs have met, they change the course of the relationship puzzle forever with regards to dating others and even participating in superficial relationships in general. It can be energetically resistive whilst attempting to form bonds with others who are not as high in frequency, and there may come a point where the endeavor to find someone new is too much of a fruitless struggle. It may be helpful to understand that the energy of I AM, once having encountered and recognized itself in the Twin, spars with the Ego, which has a challenging time actualizing the fact that the entire purpose of this incarnation is to remember who I AM, not to egoically date.

The Higher Self will force healing

As humans, we want to experience the least amount of pain as possible in our lives. After all, pain is...well, painful. Pain looks different to everyone: some find pain in change, some in stagnation; some have more physical pain than others, while some push themselves to extremes and bask in it. There is a general consensus, however, that mental pain is the worst type of anguish, and whether it's realized or not, mental anguish can be completely eradicated by understanding that it's caused solely by the Ego: the emotions that run rampant and allow the Ego to find patterns, create perceptions, and cast judgments. Of course, we're not speaking regarding mental illnesses, though it has been studied and shown that even these disorders can be lessened by the practices of mindfulness, meditation, and breathwork.

When TF separation is entered into, it is the Higher Self triggering and pushing buttons in order to get the Ego to slow down in thought, grow in higher awareness, and remember who I AM. After all, in everyday life, when things are running fairly smoothly or have become routine, what exactly is being learned? Issues that occur on the 3D plane like looming mortgage payments or picking the kids up from after school activities, or whether you're up for a promotion you think you deserve, are all rooted in perception and societal expectations.

All of these things may be your "reality," but none of them are real. This is why a TF may show up while you're married, as well, because you are stuck in stagnant energy, not growing or expanding, and accepting complacency.

3D life gets busy and makes it difficult to take or make the time to be mindful every minute of every day, work on your own healing, and ask the questions that need to be asked in order to gain more insight into your spiritual journey. When separation from the TF occurs, both Twins are triggered, and these triggers are what help to shock the Ego enough to *want* change. For the Chaser, they want separation to end so badly, that they may begin their healing just so they can come back together with their Twin in the 3D. Therefore, the Higher Self has literally forced the Ego into begin healing by putting distance between the physical Twins. For the Runner, mirroring and triggering within the 3D relationship with the Chaser was too much for them to bear, and so the Higher Self again came in and forced the room needed for the Runner to heal and grow. The Runner must have an Ego Degradation in order to come into physical, 3D "union" with the Twin, and they can only have this Ego Degradation while in separation.

When we meet our TF, although we are experiencing them on the 3D material plane at first, our 5D self is pushing to break through. We have no conscious choice during the first stages of connection, which is why there are bursts of creativity, interjections of love, mirroring, and triggers. Without these things, the Runner running would simply be a break-up, and no other thought would be put into it. But when the connection energy not only persists, but in fact gets *stronger* upon separation, we begin looking for "reasons" as to why we're feeling this way and experiencing these things. Whether it's called a Twin Flame; Karmic; Soulmate; Soul Tribe Member; Mirror Soul; Catalyst Flame; or the plethora of other terms circulating out there, in the end, it doesn't matter what the label is. You've now met a 3D manifestation that you have created in order to recognize I AM. And with those feelings of 5D connection, plus the intuition and connective signs shown during separation, it's finally understood that there is something we've been missing by solely focusing on Ego.

Since the Runner is not communicating nor participating in anything with the Chaser during separation, the Chaser also becomes desperate to interact with the TF. During separation, the best way of doing this is via the 5D. If you've met your TF in this incarnation, I'm sure you know what I'm referring to: having conversations with them in your head; meditating to connect; dreams in which you interact; and sending out loving energy so they know you're there with them. It's so very common for this to be the norm during separation, yet you may be missing the entire point of it. All of the signs, synchronicities, intuition, connection energy, and unconditional love that is felt during separation from the TF, is to "prove" to your Ego by I AM that *everything is the same* and you are *always connected to your Twin*. You and your TF are the exact same thing – everything is the exact same thing – but it is the manifestation of the TF which slaps you in the face with the truth of who I AM, because you recognize yourself as the universe within them.

What is learned in separation

Within separation, both Twins learn a lot about themselves, both in the Ego and the Higher Self. To begin with the Ego, separation forces you to learn how you were or are within interpersonal relationships and shows you what you will end up wanting to change about your egoic self. This is usually done in the form of no longer having expectations: no expectations of what you want from your TF, no expectations of what you want the relationship to look like, or what you thought your "ideal match" would be. In a sense, no longer having expectations enables non-attachment, for the intention of things falls by the wayside next to just wanting to be around the energy of the TF. It is usually during this stage that the Chaser wants to reach out to their Runner in order to tell them about their progress. It's understandable, since we've hit a milestone in which we truly have no more expectations, including whether the Runner even responds. However, that desire to reach out to the TF in order to "let them know," is a sense of pride, a sense of desire, a sense of hope, push energy, and Ego. Living in a 3D society of social media where everything is easily broadcasted, we're used to being able to express our personal feats, putting them out into the ether of the internet world and seeing what happens. But if we are attempting to reach out to our Twin so that they "know that we're here for them with no expectations attached," what are we really doing? We're hoping that, that statement will sink into the Runner's subconscious and they will either confide in us, talk to us, or reach out to us in the future. This is still chaser energy and the Ego playing tricks while trying to get validation, so just be wary. There will come a point, after surrender to the journey, in which the realization that you have no expectations will be like a beautiful secret you have for yourself, because it is just the way you are instead of what you've become.

Alongside the grasping of non-attachment or lack of expectations comes the discovery that the Ego has no bearing on existence except for its false perception. This commonly comes close at hand with the recognition of what unconditional love is. The term 'unconditional love' is thrown around capriciously within many interpersonal relationships, including those with family. But how many of those relationships would feel that love unencumbered by everything, and unconfused with obligation? Separation from the TF presents love in a manner that is so deep in connection, that it surpasses the physical manifestation of them and transposes to all things and non-things everywhere. It is universal love, connected by everything and all, and felt not only for everything in existence, but stemming from and towards the creator – I AM – you. It is an awareness that everything is the same thing, the same energy, and only differentiated by your perception of contrast, a creation by the Ego. Within this recognition is the concession that if everything is the same in the core and base of existence discerned solely by a false approach, it is an impossibility for your TF not to love you just as unconditionally as you feel love for them. However, this epiphany can only happen during separation from the physical Twin because the consent to decisive love is not towards the 3D relationship, but rather the entire universe. By this, we understand that love is simply love, but it's the expressions of love that are differentiated by Ego.

Conclusively, separation showcases the importance of what's called "Divine Timing" on a TF journey, both in 3D and 5D. Divine Timing is the Higher Self spreading, burgeoning, and budding into the Ego so that you may instill your memories of I AM into consciousness. You will recognize it since meeting the Twin and even prior, presenting to you ways in which you and your TF have been drawn towards one another this entire incarnation. As you are your TF and vice versa, the concept of manifestation is not needed to bring them back. Positive thoughts of them returning are not needed. Hopefulness, wishing, affirmations, and communicating with them on the 5D are in fact, not essential, though helpful to the mind. You are your TF – they don't exist without you. Therefore, your TF will always come back, for whatever Ego I AM placed them with, is just at attached to yours as their own. Trusting in Divine Timing is simply surrendering control to the Higher Self and acknowledging that when the Twin's Ego is ready, they will return in the 3D. At that point, you may not care whether or not they are even present in the 3D.

Realize that separation conscripts each TF party to do their own healing work. Universally, the energy of both Twins must sync up to one another, as they are 3D recognized manifestations of I AM. Both TF's mirror in 5D energy, so what one Twin raises to, the other Twin raises to, energetically. Remember that if a Twin is lower in vibrational energy, this is what caused the separation in the first place. Twins do not pull the other down vibrationally, but rather create a chasm between them physically. When the Chaser ceases chasing, the Runner has room to see themselves clearly as they have been triggered to do so by interacting with the TF. And sooner or later, both Twins realize they cannot and do not want to be with another, and so they both awaken in order to be together, whether this is conscious or not. Divine Timing enables all of these things to happen when they "should" happen, and since Divine Timing is simply the Higher Self, trust yourself.

Being in separation for both TFs is miserable. Though the Runner may appear to not care, they are working through their own traumas in order to "level up" into a higher frequency so that they can match the Chaser. As I AM energy, everything is always expanding and growing, and TFs on the 3D plane will *always* sync to the other's energy or force the Ego to begin healing. This may take quite a while, as the Ego likes to believe it's in control all the time, and in some scenarios, the Ego will never break in this manifestation. That only leads the way to repeat the same lessons in another incarnation at another point in non-existent time. If during reunion your energy begins to expand faster than the TF can keep up, you will again enter into separation. It is the responsibility of both TFs to recognize I AM energy and live accordingly. This is very akin to Soul Tribe members leaving your life when you get off of the "correct" path, and if their teachings of non-attachment have resonated, you will be able to at some point find the same non-attachment with the physicality of the Twin: aware that you are the same in every way, and therefore can never be truly separate, just as you are not separate from anything else.

False Flames

False Flames are a strange concept: one that a lot of people don't believe in, and one that is argued about regarding whether a person is a False Flame or just a Karmic masquerading as a TF. The fact is, False Flames (FFs) are one of the most interesting egoic manifestations I AM creates. They are a combination of Karmic, Soulmate, Soul Tribe, and non-Soul Family members, with attributes of the TF. However, FFs do not show up for everyone (never the Runner), and they only show up sometimes for some Egos, depending on specific factors. Therefore, they're not delineated within the Soul Family. You may or may not have a FF, you may or may not have met them prior to meeting your TF, and they are simply, like an Oracle, a 3D omen of what is to come soon. The pro to meeting a FF is that being with one can prepare you for what you are about to encounter upon meeting the TF, but the con is that they can perpetuate negative thinking and Ego, giving you more work to do upon interaction with the Twin.

When you encounter a FF, you will likely be incredibly drawn to them. And they will chase you: adamantly, fiercely, and relentlessly until you "give in." FFs function like Karmics because relationships with them are tumultuous, hard, up-and-down, and emotional. They function like Soulmates because they are completely surface and hit the Ego with desires, wants, and 3D "needs." If you are in an intimate and committed Soulmate relationship upon meeting your TF, you most likely will not encounter a FF prior (as you are already functioning in the realm of Ego with the Soulmate). FFs function like Soul Tribe Members because they may be in and out of your life for a while before you decide to be in a relationship with them. But unlike STM, a relationship with a FF will be a romantic relationship of some form, not just a friendship (though you may vacillate between the two). They will also seem very non-attached and aloof. FFs function like a non-Soul Family member because there will always be a feeling of uncertainty with them, and never a true feeling of comfortability. And the FF will show many characteristics of the TF when looking at the relationship purely on a 3D level.

You may be surprised to find that when you meet your Twin Flame, they actually remind you of your False Flame. It is very common for both the FF and the TF to look alike physically, and usually, it's your on-paper ideal of what you're physically attracted to. FFs will also be a mixture egoically of both you and your Twin. For instance, if you are patient and your TF is impulsive, your FF will present these personality traits simultaneously. They may bail from your life over and over again, giving you the impression that they're running like a TF would, but the difference is that if a FF leaves your life for a while, you won't want to or care whether you ever speak to or see them again. FFs will mirror your wants, desires, ambitions, hopes, dreams, passions, and dislikes, just like a Soulmate will. They'll actually be so similar to you egoically, that your Ego may believe that it has found "The One." But still, deep down, it won't feel "right." It won't feel comfortable being with a FF, and you may not be able to put your finger on *why* it feels that way when the Ego has been made happy. Ultimately, the Higher Self and the clairsentient understanding that something is amiss, will seep into the Ego and you will become unhappy in the relationship, even egoically. FFs also mirror your negative feeling moods and oppose your positive feeling ones. If you are depressed, the FF will also become depressed. If you are sad, they too will become sad. They will have more anger than you, but they will mirror your anger as well. And if you're excited about something, their mood will be flat or even down, sucking the energy level into lower vibrations. There is no developing self-love with a FF; in fact, the opposite occurs, whereby the Ego is running the show and makes itself feel terrible whilst being with the FF. While the saying "They made me feel this way" is always incorrect since you are one in the same as everything and it is just the mind that creates emotion, the Ego will feel that the FF has made you feel every emotion you cycle through.

How FFs present themselves is both very different and very similar from the rest of the Soul Family, because they are not part of the Soul Family. It is always easier to look at FFs through hindsight, because if encountering one, they may feel and appear to the Ego as if they are able to raise your frequency. But it is not long before you realize the FF is your shadow self in disguise; the Plutonian energy being unearthed and brought to the surface so that you may begin to acknowledge it before being thrown into the lion's den with the Twin. You and the FF will mirror each other, you will be triggered, and this is exactly why they're called False Flames; because the Ego gets attached and believes that it has met its TF. But as usual, the Ego is perceiving incorrectly. The most important thing to utilize for differentiating between a FF and a TW are the "stages" set out at the beginning of this chapter. With a FF, none of the stages will exist at the appropriate timelines, if at all.

The purpose of FFs is to portend what is to come about with the TF, both in reunion and in separation. FFs dig up the roots of your Core Karmic lesson and bring it to the forefront of your consciousness so you may recognize patterns upon meeting the TF. FFs also mirror in the 3D realm exactly how your 3D relationship with the Twin will play out, and they do this in three ways:

1. The main triggering aspect of the FF towards you will be how you and your TF first go into separation.
2. How you and your FF end the relationship is the same as what causes the last separation between you and your TF (whether you come into union after or

stay in permanent separation).

3. The FF will mirror what 3D experience your TF had, which is the majority of what needs to be healed in them.

The main triggering aspect of the FF towards you will be how you and your TF first go into separation. Whether it be through jealousy; fear of abandonment; self-sabotage; distance; difference in strong beliefs; religion; etc. The main thing that you and your FF fight about will be the exact same thing that separates you and your Twin for the first separation. It will be egoic but obviously touch upon the Core Karmic lesson with some smaller lessons sprinkled on top, most likely. If the two scenarios between your FF and your TF don't appear to be similar, go deeper. Go to the bottom of what you feel regarding both situations, and you'll see they trigger the exact same aspect of your trauma, which is most likely your Core Karmic lesson.

How you and your FF end the relationship is the same as what causes the last separation between you and your TF. Before the deciding point of whether you come into union or stay in permanent 3D separation, there will be the last separation. You may not know it's the last separation, or you may be fully aware; it depends on the situation. Whatever caused this last separation with your Twin, will be the exact same thing as what broke you and your FF up for good. It could be things like cheating; distance; lack of communication; lack of intimacy; inability for conflict resolution; etc. Whether you come into union on the 3D plane or stay permanently separated depends on how much your Ego is willing to take, and whichever you choose, is the correct answer for you.

The FF will mirror what 3D experience your TF had, which is the majority of what needs to be healed in them. This will be an identical replica between the FF and the TF. For example, if your FF was adopted and struggles with self-worth as their Core Karmic lesson, your TF will also have been adopted and struggle with the same Core Karmic lesson. If your FF had a completely absent parent which dictated their emotional standing, your TF will have dealt with the same. This is never your responsibility to "fix" or assuage, but it does give a glimpse into what the egoic issues are that will need to be overcome by the TF.

FFs will be everything you want egoically so that you attach to them in some form. However, this attachment is purely superficial and when the relationship is over, it shows you that the Ego is not what is important within a deep connection, and generally, can't be trusted. This is why Runner Twins do not have FFs; because they already function through the Ego prior to meeting the TF. FFs are meant to bring the hidden aspects of Ego up: things that were believed to be healed already, or things that the Chaser had just accepted as "the way it is" and ignored. Displacing this shadow-self shows the importance of the TF connection once on the journey. Since the Runner already knows their egoic shadow-self, they do not need a FF, but rather the Chaser to begin healing, as the TF is in the highest vibration.

The most incredible part of being in a relationship with a FF, is that every single Soul Family member you meet afterwards will lead you to your TF. It is the most beautiful and humbling practice to view a linear timeline on this 3D plane of how the FF catapulted your life towards your Twin; sometimes to the point where you made decisions and life choices that you normally wouldn't have made, but in the end, those life choices brought your 3D manifested Twin to you. That is a way to have egoic "proof" of the Higher Self. Furthermore, everything that ensues after you've met your FF is transpiring in Divine Timing, for Divine Timing is always the clock that links you to your Twin.

Signs of a Twin Flame

Though the other Soul Family Members have signs that vary, Twin Flames have signs that are constant. If you have met your TF, you will encounter *every single one* of these signs. Don't allow the Ego to pick and choose.

- Something that initially draws you to the person that is not egoic, and the feelings and energy are overwhelming
- A burst of creativity directly after meeting face-to-face if you are the Chaser, or possibly prior if you are the

Runner

- Romantic relationship *only*
- Immense feelings are immediate, or within one week of meeting the person. They are not drawn out over years
- Interjection of grandiosity out of nowhere within the first month of meeting, even though you cognitively may not feel the statement yet
- The first separation occurs within two months of meeting face-to-face
- An absolute obsession and rumination during the first separation over the relationship, even though you've only known them for a short period of time. Something feeling very "off." Over the next separations, the obsession begins to dwindle through your own self-work
- The beginning stages of true Ego Degradation, in which you reevaluate your entire reason for Being; "purpose;" 3D and spiritual life; how you interact with others; and habits you want to shed
- Perpetual cycles of separation and reunion that occur for no concrete reason except the Runner's justifications as to why the TFs cannot be together
- During separation, the beginning of true self-love and universal love with no 3D reason as to why
- Continuous mindful practice, spiritual growth, and self-healing for no other reason than for yourself
- A true and deep understanding that everything is the same, which transmutes into a cognitive and tangible practice of this concept in daily life (how you relate to

things, to others, to yourself, and to your TF)

- A true and deep realization that you are the Universe manifested in physical form, and therefore you have created everything ever in existence
- A full understanding that your Ego creates all emotions and thoughts, and nothing on the outside is dictating how you feel, think, or what happens to you
- A recognition that any form of duality is a perception of the Ego (this is very, very difficult to have your Ego remember at all times, since we function on the 3D plane of dualism)
- A deep belief and trust that the Higher Self knows and acts in your best interest
- Trusting in Divine Timing (this may be later on in your journey)

Union

Union within a Twin Flame journey is generally considered an end to separation on the 3D plane, where the TFs can be together romantically in this incarnation. However, as you and your TF are the exact same thing, it needs to be recognized that union is genuinely something completely different than being physically with the Twin. Union, in actuality, is simply remembering the fact that you are I AM and responding to it accordingly, even while in 3D separation. Union with the TF is something that occurs internally and begins to manifest externally. It is the 4D bridge from 3D to 5D, and once this bridge has been cleared of debris and consistently open for your passage to and from, you will not need to focus on anything external in order to be in true union, for you will be together and one with your true Self; the universe. If your TF reappears in the 3D, then that is just an added bonus for the Ego.

So how do we get to this point of union with I AM, what steps can we take, and what does it actually look like? The answer is non-attachment, the very thing that all Soul Family Members have been trying to show us our entire life in some way. There is a vast difference between non-attachment and detachment. To detach means to have a complete lack of interest in the world around, what is going on, or with a specific individual that you have detached from. It's an aloofness of some form, which is why the Chaser Ego believes that the Runner does not care about them, since they present an appearance of unresponsiveness. Non-attachment on the other hand, is a consistent practice of mindfulness, egoic steadiness, and presence in the current moment. To be non-attached means to be equanimous; to no longer have a desire for a specific outcome; to not allow the Ego and all of its waves to cause reactions or fluctuations in peace. The term for non-attachment in Sanskrit is *Vairagya*, which means "without personal desires." In order to not have personal desires, we must pay continuous attention to the Ego and make sure it does not destroy its own serenity.

In order to reach non-attachment within the TF journey specifically, there must first come acceptance by both parties during separation: acceptance that you and your TF are currently over in the 3D; acceptance that there was a Third Party Situation; acceptance that there is distance, or that one of you is married, or that they don't want to speak with you at this moment. Acceptance that all of the things you wanted to say but never got to say will go unheard for now; or acceptance that you lost control of your temper the last time you saw one another. Whatever it is that is that has your Ego scrambling for answers as to why; what; when; how; should have; could have; wanted to; don't want; didn't want, is the mind refusing to accept what has transpired in the 3D and holding onto dualistic precepts. But guess what? It *did* transpire. It's already happened in our 3D perceived linear timeline, and there's no amount of wishing or beating yourself up about it that can manifest you going back and changing what has already taken place. But acceptance doesn't mean you have to be all right with what has occurred. Acceptance is not defeat. Acceptance is purely self-compassion and the statement of "Okay, this is where I'm at, and that's the right place to be for now." Acceptance takes more grace, humanity towards the self, and self-tenderness than anything else, because if we've manifested a TF in this incarnation, we're already dealing with the Core Karmic lesson of self-worth or self-love, and to be compassionate towards oneself is a very difficult task.

Once acceptance has occurred, the next step towards non-attachment is surrender: surrender to Divine Timing; surrender to everything that has arisen; surrender to the knowledge that no matter how much you try to "cut the cord" or "break the bond," there is no escaping your Twin, because your Twin is you. Surrender to the feeling of connection energy; to being on a higher vibrational plane than those around you; to feeling misunderstood all the time and acknowledging that it's just the Ego wanting to be understood, for energy cannot and does not delineate. Surrendering to the Higher Self, which works in your best interest at all times; and possibly most difficult, surrendering control over to the universe. Within this abdication of control, the Ego begins to become aware that not everything it perceives is correct, since perception of negativity may have the alternate outcome; fear can become lessons; and joy can be observed as fleeting. Mindfulness expands, and you may live this life in a perpetual state of objective observation, non-attached to what is ensuing, and equanimous in what eventuates. This steady existence of mind grants the ability to truly let go of any desired outcome with regards to the 3D physicality of the TF, which continues even if the Twins are physically together.

It is common for TF Chasers to worry that if they surrender and focus solely on themselves and their own journey, that their Runner Twin will feel neglected, detached, and therefore, not reach out...this is Ego. This has nothing to do with non-attachment, for we are not speaking of mental or energetic detachment from the Twin, but rather an imperturbable mind frame. When you can reach a state of *Vairagya*, the entirety of the TF journey opens up to you, and you begin experiencing it on a completely euphoric level, even without the physicality of the TF present.

With non-attachment, you can read the signs along your path with true awareness and understanding instead of desire, hope, and irritation. There is no longer an obsession with seeing repeating numbers, or what are believed to be synchronicities pointing back to the TF everywhere you look. If repeating numbers are consistently seen, you thank the Higher Self for reminding you it's always there. If a synchronicity is glaringly obvious, you smile and acknowledge that you're forever connected because you're the same thing. Life ceases being hard getting through with small "annoyances" supposedly pointing towards the TF, and instead becomes ripe with the awareness of interconnectedness.

With non-attachment, you can heal things within yourself as they surface instead of having to retroactively work on them or needing to take the time to dig them up in order to better understand your actions, reflexes, triggers, and reactions. When you are non-attached to things, you are more apt to feel the transitions of the planets and their ability to do the work for you, surfacing anything that your Ego doesn't want to deal with, and having the clarity of mind to work through them instead of suppressing them. If the Ego gets triggered by a Soul Family member or a Karmic lesson, the beautiful objectivity of non-attachment allows you to look at that trigger with empathy and compassion for yourself in order to figure out why you are being triggered, observe any patterns, and change the course of your neural pathways with pure consciousness. Hypnotherapy, Cognitive Behavioral Therapy, and meditation become more competent, since the Ego is less attached to its perceived outcome. And with non-attachment to thoughts, you can view them justly and possibly with enthusiasm at how your Ego functions. You no longer have to be scared about your own brain's dominance over you, but instead keep it leashed and under control simply by studying it dispassionately.

The most sublime function of non-attachment is the sense of peace and connection with yourself and everything. Most importantly, you stop looking for reassurance, approval, validation, worth, and love in anything external, since you remember that everything is One, and therefore, everything is *you*. And if everything is you, the false egoic notions people place on top of the true Self has no bearing on how your Ego feels about itself, and no merit whatsoever. Therefore, you look inward, because as I AM, nothing can be more true than what is already swirling inside of you.

Two more things

A lot of my clients come to me believing they're on a Twin Flame journey and get very distressed when I tell them that they're not, but rather dealing with a Soulmate or Soulmate + Karmic. I've heard statements such as "...but I want them to be my Twin Flame!" or "I really want to meet my Twin Flame," or "How do I manifest my Twin Flame?" And I continuously tell them this: *do not wish to be on a TF journey if you're not.* If you are desiring to be on a TF journey, you are simply thinking with the Ego and not understanding the absolute pain that a TF journey can cause when you're going through it. Anyone who is actually on a TF journey will validate this point, since most want to get off the ride. It's a cyclical carousel of Ego Degradation, pain, submission, acceptance, healing, dealing with the out-of-control Ego, and not being able to function "normally" within society anymore since everyone thinks you've lost your mind. It's isolating, confusing, and painful to be on a TF journey, and though the end result (if you allow your Ego to get there) is a beautiful outcome, it's much more peaceful to remember that you are I AM without the added hindrance of a TF relationship.

Though TFs are a "Fast Pass" to recognizing yourself as I AM, they come with a plethora of egoic struggles, hardships, and life changes whether we're ready for them or not. You are able to heal your Core Karmic lesson without a TF aiding you, and you are able to reach the pinnacle of this incarnation's awakening if you do it on your own. You just have to be more mindful about getting there. In a TF journey, the Ego does not have a choice in breaking down, and it can cause a lot of chaos around you and within you. You are the one who chose to manifest your Soul Family members in this incarnation based upon what your Ego can handle and what lessons you need to learn. Don't desire something "more" because your Ego is telling you that that's what it wants. You are on the right path for you, and as everything is the same, you are experiencing TFs via different Egos already.

I get a lot of questions regarding whether a TF can be a friend, parent, child, sister, etc. The answer is "no." TFs are *always* only romantic relationships, and this is because a TF needs to hit on our Ego in a way where it becomes dismantled. Imagine how it would appear if your child was a Twin Flame; who is the Runner and who is the Chaser? If your child continuously ran, there would be no self-development, but rather self-deprecation constructed by the Ego as to why you're "a bad parent." If your brother was a TF, it would be too societally awkward for you to have the "stages" spoken about earlier. Your Ego would never allow it to happen because we have been programmed in this way. Not to mention, TFs are "activated" within a week of meeting one another. This isn't going to happen as an infant or toddler.

When we think of the most unbounded 3D love, we reminisce about *Romeo & Juliet*, *Tristan & Isolde*, Heathcliff and Catherine Earnshaw, Jack and Rose, and Noah and Allie. These are the loves that the Ego desires most, and these are the types of love stories that make you want to throw caution to the wind and change everything in order to make it work. I'm not saying that any of these fictitious characters were meant to be portrayed as TFs (though there are no doubt viewers and readers who believe this tumultuous, Karmic love is the end all, be all). The point is that it is only a love that can stab the heart in every which way that will ultimately push Ego to grow and expand as much as necessary to fully remember I AM. This isn't to say that if you have not manifested a TF in this life that you cannot remember who I AM; some Twins will remain in chaser or runner energy for the rest of this incarnation because they cannot transpose the Ego. TFs are simply a "Fast Pass" to breaking down the Ego quicker than if you choose to walk the path alone, however, they pose significantly more work than those doing it without a manifested Twin. Any Soul Family member can trigger the Ego to the point of breaking, but if the Core Karmic lesson is still not healed, the Ego will always find a way to mold and reshape itself in order to function on this 3D plane of reality. It is always your own responsibility to move yourself forward, grow, expand, and heal, and whether you do that alone, with a Karmic, a Soulmate, a Soul Tribe Member, or a Twin Flame, is completely up to you. But regardless of whatever title perceived or placed on other Egos who have affected your life significantly, the end result is always the same: *they were all just...you.*

The Importance of Astrology

The lessons we have decided to learn throughout our unending manifestations are immense, all stemming from the Core Karmic lesson. Luckily, we have a blueprint to guide us to what those, and the symptom Karmic lessons will be in our current incarnation. Our natal chart is a key to remembering what we manifested in this body to learn, and to remind us that we are One with I AM. You as the universe chose to come here as a human on Earth during this fictitious time frame, with whatever world events are happening. You chose to manifest with your parents and created the people around you to help deliver the lessons you wanted to learn in this specific lifetime.

No matter your thoughts on astrology, your natal chart tells you what needs to be cultivated, what you have already learned, and gives you a guide of how certain elements of this manifestation will play out. Your natal chart can tell you why you follow certain patterns in your life regarding relationships, money, values, home life, etc. It can show you specific years or cycles in your life where you will have more issues with distinct elements, or what you will be continuously working against in this incarnation. It will also show specific years or cycles in your life where you will have an easier time with certain elements. You can use it to compare against your Soul Family's charts to pinpoint what they are meant to teach you. You can use it to look back and identify areas in your past that stand out to you and see what planetary transits during that period were showing you. And you can even use it to determine lessons you have learned in previous manifestations.

If you do not have nor have ever had access to your exact birth information for whatever reason, then that in itself is probably one of the main lessons for you in this manifestation: to trust the universe, yourself, and whatever emotions come up for you without trying to control too much.

Knowing your planetary placements from when you were born will help you maneuver through this life less in the fog of your own Ego, and it will explain why the Ego tends to get more riled up at certain times, dependent on planetary transits. The natal chart is a very underutilized tool that can aid in this life's journey and help to remember I AM.

Please note that I am not an astrologer, nor do I claim to be one. I have been an avid student of astrology since I was little, and can read charts and figure out the meaning of transits by hearing about them, but to get a full picture and understanding of your own chart, it is important that you either learn how to read it yourself, or go to a professional astrologer. To begin with, there are a ton of online tools that will give you your chart and an overview of it just by putting in your birth information. All things spoken about in this chapter correlate to Western Tropical Astrology. Please remember to get the time of your birth as accurately as possible, since this delineates your Ascendant sign and the houses that each of the planets and signs were in. Here are some things you can look at in your chart and what they might tell you:

General traits of the signs

Get to know the general traits of each zodiac sign, both the "positive" and "negative" attributes. For example, a Taurus' "positive" attributes would be loyalty, steadfastness, and being grounded, whereas their "negative" attributes would be stubbornness, materialism, and hard-headedness. These attributes will help you to understand the 'themes' of where each planetary placement or transit occurs; what type of Soul Family members you attract into your life; what types of Egos you innately get along with or don't; attributes you need to learn or overcome; and how certain characteristics of your Ego's personality comes through. It's also good to note what planets rule each sign, so taking the example of Taurus again, which is ruled by Venus, we can see how those with a Sun in Taurus love beauty, creature comforts, and monetary gains.

"The Big 3"

The Sun sign, Rising sign (also called Ascendant), and Moon sign give the general overview to the Ego. The Sun sign is who the Ego is at its core, so if your Sun is in Leo, you're gregarious, like to be the center of attention, and are feisty. The Sun sign can give you a hint as to what your Core Karmic lesson is, so if we take the same Leo Sun, it points towards either a Core Karmic lesson of self-worth or non-attachment, dependent on how the characteristics play out. The Ascendant is the mask we wear when we're in society. For example, if the Ascendant is a Leo, we *portray* ourselves as gregarious, the center of attention, and feisty, though dependent on what the Sun sign is, we might not actually feel that way. The Ascendant is important to view how other Egos portray us, especially the Soul Family. If we're dealing with a Karmic, they may view our Ascendant portrayal as what should be attacked, not paying attention to our Sun and Moon signs; just as we would view the same with them. Or, a Soulmate may see past our Ascendant characteristics, making us feel like they truly "know" us. Lastly, the Moon sign are the Ego's propensity towards emotions and how we feel about our own Ego. Therefore, a Leo Moon would signify that the Ego has a deep sense of dignity and expectations of respect from others. With this moon placement alone, we see that the Core Karmic lesson could be of self-worth or self-love, since we expect others to give us those things, and turn outwards for the feelings we would like to feel about ourself.

Personal planets

The personal planets are Mercury, Venus, and Mars; all of the planets closest to us and on the inside of the asteroid belt that cuts through our Solar System. Mercury is how we communicate, Venus is how we are in relationships, and Mars is how we fight and take action. If you have a Mercury in Virgo, for example, your communication may be cold and distant, but succinct. If your Venus is in Libra, you view relationships as needing to be balanced, yet probably always are in unbalanced relationships. Also, since Libra is naturally ruled by the sign Venus, love and relationships are most likely very important to you. And if your Mars is in Gemini, your ways of arguing and taking action can be like the twins that the sign represents: sometimes fiery and fierce, and sometimes soft and gentle. These characteristics will allow you to see how you interact with Soul Family members, and the dualistic attributes of each sign synced up with the planets will give you a better overview of how your Ego is portrayed outwardly, and what it needs to find non-attachment with.

The Houses

There are twelve Houses in astrology that correlate with each twelve zodiac signs. Where your Ascendant lay is in the first House (the horizon), and correlates to the Egoic self. So for example, if your Ascendant is Scorpio, your second House will be Sagittarius, third Capricorn, fourth Aquarius, and so on, going in order of the zodiac wheel. Each House represents a different aspect of life (values, communication, day-to-day work, higher knowledge, health, etc.). Alongside this, each House is ruled by a zodiac sign naturally, beginning with Aries as the first House and ending with Pisces as the twelfth House, since Aries is the first zodiac sign, and Pisces is the last. Where the signs are in your Houses can help to show you certain areas of your life that may cause more struggles, and others that may come easily. For example, if you have Virgo in the second House of values, you may value practicality and steadiness ("positive" aspect of Virgo) but also value shallow concepts such as money, looks, and creature comforts ("negative" aspect of Virgo).

Houses are incredibly important to see how and when things will happen in your life. For example, if there is a lunar eclipse occurring in Virgo which rules your second House, something will come to fruition or be uncovered regarding your value system. A Karmic lesson, most likely. If in the natal chart a House does not have any planets within it, you have already learned the lessons associated with that House in a previous incarnation. This also is true if there are many planets in one House; in this incarnation, that will be a big theme for you to learn, or will express to you another way of looking at your Egoic life "purpose." The Houses are equivalent to a crystal ball letting you know the dates and times things will occur and in which area of your life.

Nodes, outer planets, aspects

The North Node and the South Node, also called the "Nodes of Fate," are not actual bodies of matter, but rather astronomical points in the sky. The Nodes change every eighteen months, and your particular Nodes when you were born led you towards something and away from something else. The North Node is where you're headed, and it will be delineated by the House and sign that it was in during your birth. The South Node is where you're coming from, and it will be exactly opposite to the North Node. So if the North Node is in Gemini in the third House, the South Node will be in Sagittarius in the seventh house. The Nodes can tell you what your interests will be, what your Ego struggles to let go of, what your Egoic "purpose" is, and how you will relate to another Ego on a deeper level. If you have the same Nodes as someone you believe is your Twin Flame, even if they're in different Houses, this will point to the same Core Karmic lesson.

The outer planets (Saturn, Uranus, Pluto, Neptune, Jupiter) will show you aspects of your natal chart that you will have abundance in and detriment. Outer planets are called "generational planets" because they're so slow moving, that they tend to encompass a large group of people, all having the same placement in their natal chart. Outer planets not only point to mass Karmic lessons, but also societal issues that will come up during this incarnation. With all planets, we look at aspects, which are when two or more planets interact with one another. They can do things like trine, oppose, quincunx, square, conjunct, eclipse, retrograde, lunar cycle, etc. Whatever aspects you have in your natal chart will influence how these planets work for you in this incarnation, and whatever aspects planets make during their day-to-day transits will also affect how your Ego perceives everything. When outer planets aspect with personal planets, they affect us more intimately (i.e. Jupiter square Mercury), and when outer planets aspect other outer planets, we tend to feel them on a global scale (i.e. Saturn conjunct Uranus). All planets and all aspects will generally affect us in some way since we are made of the same thing, and dependent on what area of your chart the transit is happening is where it will affect your life. Planetary transits can portray new Soul Family members who are about to enter; members who are about to leave; when relationships that have run their course will dissipate; when we're going to move, or change jobs, or get married. They can show us when we're going to have Ego Degradation symptoms in specific parts of our life, or why it was so hard for us to fit in as a child. But in order to get this information, you must know your natal chart so you can see how transits and aspects exactly affect your current Ego and how you can begin breaking it down.

It's important to look at the entire picture of the natal chart, and not just the Sun sign. Your Ego is a convoluted and tangled web of beautiful contradictions, and with every placement in the natal chart, a different aspect of the Ego is born. You manifested I AM into this human body shell with very specific planetary placements and transits that you are physically, mentally, and energetically part of, and those planets are reminding your Ego that there is something so much greater than its tiny belief system; the Higher Self's power, coursing through every atom of your body. Every single human incarnation has a Core Karmic lesson they are currently grappling with. Though I AM has created all and all is unanimous, each Ego must experience itself in different ways in order to truly learn the lessons. It's important and extremely helpful to identify your Core Karmic lesson in this Ego, for it will aid in understanding how the Ego moves through this manifestation and what it attempts to get you to believe. Once the Core Karmic lesson is determined, it's easier to notice the Karmic symptoms and the triggers for them, and these can most likely be seen in the natal chart. Recognizing that everything is One and you have created all will benefit the healing process so that you can find more equanimity in all things, and finally rejoin the Cosmos as the true Self without the strain of Ego. And to assist in this endeavor, you have given yourself an astrological natal chart and Soul Family to advise the Ego and help you remember that you are literally the universe manifested in physical form.

References

Beall, A. *Wired Magazine*; "Theory Claims to Offer the First 'Evidence' Our Universe is a Hologram." January 31, 2017. Wired.co.uk/article/our-universe-is-a-hologram

Brenner, L. *Sciencing*; "What is the Fifth Dimension?" December 6, 2020. Sciencing.com/characteristics-gravity-8589279.html

CERN Accelerating Science; "The Standard Model." Home.cern/science/physics/standard-model

Chown, M. *Science Focus Magazine*; "Our Universe May Have a Fifth Dimension That Would Change Everything We Know About Physics." November 4, 2021. Sciencefocus.com/space/fifth-dimension/

Clark, S. *The Guardian*; "Lost in Space? A Brief Guide to the 'Holographic Principle' of the Universe." January 31, 2017. Theguardian.com/science/shortcuts/2017/jan/31/guide-to-holographic-principle-of-universe

Clavin, W. *Caltech Magazine*; "Untangling Quantum Entanglement." Fall, 2019. Magazine.caltech.edu/post/untangling-entanglement

Colvin, C. & Fliers, P. *The Conversation*; "How the US Government Seized all Citizens' Gold in 1930s." May 21, 2020. Theconversation.com/how-the-us-government-seized-all-citizens-gold-in-1930s

Dillbeck, M.C.; Landrith, G; Orme-Johnson, D.W. *Journal of Criminal Justice*; "Transcendental Meditation Program and Crime Rate Change in a Sample of Forty-Eight Cities." 1981. Volume 4, 25-45.

Emspak, J. *Space.com*; "Quantum Entanglement: a Simple Explanation." March 15, 2022. Space.com/31933-quantum-entanglement-action-at-a-distance.html

Headrick, M. & Goodman, L. (Host). *Brande is NOW* podcast; "The Theory that the Universe is a Hologram Explained in Under 5 Minutes." November 16, 2018. Brandeis.edu/now/2018/november/ thetake-podcast-hologram.html

Keim, B. *Wired Magazine*; "Everywhere in a Flash: the Quantum Physics of Photosynthesis." February 3, 2010. Wired.com/2010/02/quantum-photosynthesis/

Morris, A. *Phys.org*; "Experiment Demonstrates Quantum Mechanical Effects from Biological Systems." December 5, 2017. phys.org/news/2017-12-quantum-mechanical-effects-biological.html

Moseman, A. *Discover Magazine*; "Quantum Leaf? Algae Uses Physics Trick to Boost Photosynthesis Efficiency." February 4, 2010.   Discovermagazine.com/planet-earth/quantum-leaf-algae-use-physics-trick-to-boost-photosynthesis-efficiency

Perkowitz, S. *Encyclopaedia Britannica*; "$E=mc^2$ equation." Britannica.com/science/E-mc2-equation

Selbie, J. *Science & Nonduality*; "Quantum Coherence and the Hidden Secret Behind Our Bodies." Scienceandnonduality.com/article/quantum-coherence-and-the-hidden-secret-behind-our-bodies

Shah, S. *Thrive Global*; "The Undeniable Power of Mass Meditation: 3 Top Reasons You Wanna Try It." Thriveglobal.com/stories/the-undeniable-power-of-mass-meditation-3-top-reasons-you-wanna-try-it/

Sundermier, A. *Energy.gov*; "The Particle Physics of You." November 6, 2015. Energy.gov/articles/particle-physics-you

Sutter, P. *Live Science*; "What is Quantum Entanglement?" May 26, 2021. Livescience.com/what-is-quantum-entanglement.html

Trimarchi, M. *How Stuff Works* (PDF); "What Caused the Dust Bowl?" Fldoe.org/core/fileparse.php/7539/urlt/Mod4-H14.pdf

University of New South Wales. *Phys.org*; "Quantum Biology: Algae Evolved to Switch Quantum Coherence on and off." June 16, 2014. Phys.org/news/2014-06-quantum-biology-algae-evolved-coherence.html

Wood, C. *Space.com*; "What is Quantum Gravity?" August 27, 2019. Space.com/quantum-gravity.html

www.ingramcontent.com/pod-product-compliance
Lightning Source LLC
Chambersburg PA
CBHW072041150726
47996CB00014B/202